The Qaba
Light:
The Occult Qabalah
Reclaimed

By G. M. Jaron[1]

---

[1] Gary M. Jaron can be reached at gmjaron@uw.edu and my blog is garyjaron.com

First published 2018
Revised in 2019

Printed by CreateSpace, Charleston South Carolina, U.S.A.
CreateSpace is a DBA of On-Demand Publishing LLC, part of the Amazon
group of companies.

ISBN-13:978-0692054864

Gary M. Jaron can be reached at **gmjaron@uw.edu**
Blogs: **http://garyjaron.com/**

Cover Illustration is taken from the cover page of the 1516 Latin translation
Portae Lucis of Rabbi Gikatilla's circa 1290 *Sha'are Orah, Gates of Light. The
source of the picture was the Center for Online Judaic Studies.*

This book uses the Palatino Linotype font. This selection was based on the
font used in my hardback edition of Ray Bradbury's *Dandelion Wine.*

Table of Contents

Table of Figures

Chronology of selected events in the Western World

The purpose of this timeline is to give the history of the Kabballah and the Occult a context; it is to answer the question: what else was going on in the Western World at those times? The dates of events occurring in BCE are the best guesses of current scholars. For the BCE events, I will simply relate significant events in the history of the Hebrews who become the Judeans. Overall, no causality between the events listed is implied. Any meaning and significance you find is all the process of your own mind when it encounters synchronicity. Lastly, the timeline ends with a bit of shameless self-promotion.

1025-1005 BCE Saul is the king of the Hebrews

1005-960/5 David is the king of the Hebrews

965-928 or 960-925: King Solomon. The building of the Temple in Jerusalem, asserting a single Temple for a religion of single God of Judah, Hebrews become Judeans.

928/925-722 Divided Kingdoms of Judah and Israel

722 Northern Kingdom of Israel conquered by Assyria Empire.

720: Exile of upper levels of society to Assyria, this event is recorded in the history of the Judeans as the myth of the 10 lost tribes.

597: First Capture of Jerusalem by Babylon & first Babylonian Exile.

587/6 Recapture/2nd Capture of Jerusalem by Babylon & Destruction of 1st Temple.

597-586: Babylonian Exile, The beginning of *Judaism*, something different than the Kingdom of Judah, imagining YHWH as the sole creator of the world. The *Soferim* (the scribes) record the stories of the Hebrews and the Judeans and possibly create and write the books of the Torah, Joshua, and Judges.

539: Fall of Babylonian empire to the Persian empire.

538 Edict of Cyrus of Persia allowing Judean exiles to return. Now there are two groups of power within the Judeans, the ex-royal court and ex-temple group and the Scribes who are the proto-Rabbis, the birth of rabbinic religion with a group of people living in Jerusalem and Babylon.

520: Dedication of the rebuilding of the 2nd Temple in Jerusalem.

458 Priest Ezra comes to Jerusalem, the reading from the *Torah*. Ezra brings from Babylon a copy of the *Torah* (?). *"A Talmudic story, perhaps referring to an earlier time, relates that three Torah scrolls were found in the Temple court but were at variance with each other. The differences were then resolved by majority decision among the three."* [For a discussion see: Zeitlin, S. (April 1966), Were There Three Torah-Scrolls in the Azarah? The Jewish Quarterly Review New Series, 56(4), 269–272}

430-330 Writing of the books of Ezra & Nehemiah & Chronicles

301-198 Jerusalem under Ptolemaic control (Egypt-based Hellenists). The time of Philo of Alexandria of Egypt. Between 430 -190, the full collection of texts of what will be called the canon of the Hebrew bible the *TaNaK* must have been finished.

250 Septuagint project: the translation of the 'Hebrew Bible' into Greek variants by Alexandrian scholars. *"The Talmud and Karaite manuscript state that a standard copy of the Hebrew Bible was kept in the court of the Temple in Jerusalem for the benefit of copyists; there were paid correctors of Biblical books among the officers of the Temple (Talmud, tractate Ketubot 106a). This text is mentioned in The Letter of Aristeas, called so because it was a letter addressed from Aristeas to his brother Philocrates, deals primarily with the reason the Greek translation of the Hebrew Law, also called the Septuagint, was created, as well as the people and processes involved. The letter's author alleges to be a courtier of Ptolemy II Philadelphus (reigned 281-246 BCE)."* [Wikipedia]

198-167+ Seleucids (Syrian based Hellenists) control of Jerusalem Territory

167 Maccabean Revolt against the Seleucids who desecrated the 2nd

Temple.

164: Recapture & rededication of 2nd Temple by Maccabees

164-42? Judean Religion revival & ascendency over 'Rabbis' by Maccabean Hasmonean Priest-Kings. The invention of Monotheism 'One True God' during this time?

157–129 Hasmonean dynasty establishes its royal dominance in Judea during the renewed war with Seleucid Empire. In the later part of the Second Temple period (2nd century BC), the Second Commonwealth of Judea (Hasmonean Kingdom) was established and religious matters were determined by a pair (zugot) which led the Sanhedrin.

70 Hillel becomes the president of the Sanhedrin in Jerusalem.

45-44- Cicero's philosophical works. Julius Caesar was assassinated. Factional strife for control of Roman rule of Palestine

40 Roman Senate appoints Herod, aka the great, King of Judea

37 Herod conquers Galilee, Judea, and Jerusalem from Hasmonean Priest-King

CE

4 CE- 39 Rules of Herod Antipas, a son of Herod the Great.

10 Hillel the Elder dies, leading to the dominance of Shammai till 30

29/30 Death of Jesus of Nazarene executed.

35 Paul of Tarsus sees Jesus in mystical vision on the road to Damascus.

40-44 Rule of Herod Agrippa, grandson of Herod the Great. Philo of Alexandria flourishes; he provides the integration of Judean and proto-Jewish religious thinking and Platonism, developing/creating Biblical commentary on the Biblical text, blending Jewish Deity with the Greek concept of Logos.

44 Emperor Claudius returns Palestine to Roman provincial status.

44-66 Unrest in Palestine by Judeans and Pharisee's instigators.

48 Council of Apostles at Jerusalem recognizes Paul's mission to Gentiles.

50-60 Letters of Paul composed

60 For the Romans to complete the conquest of the Isles of Britain they believed they had to break the power of the Druids. The Druids center was the isle of Anglesey. The Roman general Gaius Suetonius Paulinus crossed the Menai Strait, to attack the druids who had rallied in their stronghold of the Island of Mona (Anglesey) off the mainland of North Wales. On the island, the Druids made their last stand against the conquering legions of Rome. Tacitus left a description of the Battle of Anglesey / Mona:-'On the shore stood the opposing army with its densest array of armed warriors. Between the ranks dashed women, attired in black like the Furies with their hair disheveled, waving burning brands. All around them were Druids lifting up their hands to heaven and pouring forth dreadful implications. Our soldiers were so petrified by the unfamiliar sight that as if their limbs were paralyzed, they stood motionless, exposed to wounds. Until at last, urged by their general not to quail before a troop of frenzied women, they bore the standards onwards, smote down all resistance, and wrapped the foe in the flames of his own brands.' After their victory at the battle of Mona, many of the druids were massacred, no quarter was given, and the shrine and the sacred groves were destroyed. [http://www.englishmonarchs.co.uk/celts_5.html]. Paulinus's forces then had to leave Anglesey in response to Queen Boudica and her forces. She was the queen of the British Celtic Iceni tribe, and she was leading the uprising against the occupying forces of the Roman Empire. Although she led her forces in initial successes, ultimately her army was defeated in the Battle of Watling Street. This open revolt and crisis caused Nero to consider withdrawing all Roman forces from Britain, but Suetonius Paulinus' eventual victory over Boudica confirmed Roman control of the province of Britain.

May 66: Procurator Florus desecrates Temple and then rebels led by Eleasar, son of the High Priest, occupies Temple.

66-70: The Great Jewish Revolt against Roman occupation ended with the destruction of the Second Temple and the fall of Jerusalem. 1,100,000 people are killed by the Romans during the siege, and 97,000 were captured and enslaved. The Sanhedrin was relocated to Yavneh by Yochanan ben Zakkai, see also Council of Jamnia. Fiscus Judaicus levied on all Jews of the Roman Empire whether they aided the revolt or not.

64-68 Apostles Peter and Paul were killed in Rome by Nero's rule.

70: Jerusalem Temple razed by Rome. Thus ends the power base of Priest who became the Sadducees. They compete with the Pharisees Rabbis and their ascendency, Triumph of Judaism. Rabbi Yochanan Ben Zakkai gets permission, according to Rabbinic legend, to build a 'school' in the city of Yavneh. The start of Mishnah in an Oral form that leads to the creation of the Talmud in written form. Rabbinic Judaism is now the only power base. The Rule of Rabbinic/Talmudic Constitutional Law of the Jewish People.

Following the destruction of the Temple, Rome governed Judea through a Procurator at Caesarea and a Jewish Patriarch. A former leading Pharisee, Yochanan ben Zakkai, was appointed the first Patriarch (the Hebrew word, Nasi, also means prince or president), and he re-established the Sanhedrin at Yavneh under Pharisee control. Instead of giving tithes to the priests and sacrificing offerings at the Temple, the rabbis instructed Jews to give money to charities and study in local Synagogues, as well as to pay the Fiscus Iudaicus. The Merkavah (Chariot metaphor taken from the book of Ezekiel) riders, a form of Jewish Mysticism flourishes among a select group of Rabbis. The legend of the four who ventured to PaRDeS (the Garden aka paradise aka the heavenly throne), amongst those four was Rabbi Akiva. The invention of the dual Torah system, the Written Text of the Torah (and the rest of the Scriptures), and the Oral Torah (the teachings of the Rabbis). The legend of Oral Torah at Sinai. This story explains why the Rabbis have the authority to decide and interpret the Torah. The story of how the revelation and authority to interpret the Law was passed down in Oral Tradition from Moses to the Rabbis. All that the Rabbis would write and teach was given at Sinai, so the story goes.

70–200 Period of the Tannaim, rabbis who organized and elucidated the Jewish oral law. The decisions of the Tannaim are contained in the Mishnah, Baraita, Tosefta, and various Midrash compilations. *Somewhere during this time, the Sefer Yetzirah was written. "The historical origin of the Sefer Yetzirah was placed by Reitzenstein (Poimandres, p. 291) in the 2nd century BCE. According to Christopher P. Benton, the Hebrew grammatical form places its origin closer to the period of the Mishna, around the 2nd century CE."* [Wikipedia]

73 Final events of the Great Jewish Revolt – the fall of Masada. Christianity starts off as a Jewish sect and then develops its own texts and ideology and branches off from Judaism to become a distinct religion.

132: Emperor Hadrian threatened to rebuild Jerusalem as a pagan city dedicated to Jupiter, called Aelia Capitolina. Some of the leading sages of the Sanhedrin supported a rebellion (and, for a short time, an independent state) led by Simon bar Kozeba (also called Bar Kochbah, or "son of a star"); some, such as Rabbi Akiva, believed Bar Kochbah to be messiah or king. Up until this time, many Christians were still part of the Jewish community. However, they did not support or take part in the revolt. Whether because they had no wish to fight, or because they could not support a second messiah in addition to Jesus, or because of their harsh treatment by Bar Kochbah during his brief reign, these Christians also left the Jewish community around this time.

135: This revolt ended when Bar Kochbah and his army were defeated. The Romans then barred Jews from Jerusalem.

136 Rabbi Akiva executed by the Romans

138 With Emperor Hadrian's death, the persecution of Jews within the Roman Empire is eased and Jews are allowed to visit Jerusalem on Tisha B' Av. In the following centuries, the Jewish center moves to Galilee.

951 Rabbi Saadia Gaon writes the first commentary to the Sefer Yetzirah.

1040 Shlomo Yitzhak, who will become Rabbi Shlomo Yitzhak and known as RASHI is born in Troyes France.

1095 The first of the Papal sanctioned Christian and Islamic wars initiated by Pope Urban II by declaring the first Crusade.

Circa 1101- 1200 Provence France School of Kabbalah. The possible timeframe for the writing of *the Bahir.* *"The historical critical study of this book points to a later date of composition. For some time scholars believed that it was written in the 13th century by Isaac the Blind, or by those in his school. The first sentence, "And now men see not the light which is bright in the skies" (Job 37:21), being isolated, and having no connection with what follows, was taken to be an allusion to the blindness of its author. However, modern scholars of Kabbalah now hold that at least part of the Bahir was an adaptation of an older work, the Sefer Raza Rabba. This older book is mentioned in some of the works of the Geonim; however no complete copies of Sefer Raza Rabba are still in existence. However, quotes from this book can still be found in some older works. Scholar Ronit Meroz argues that elements in the Bahir date back to 10th century Babylonia, as witnessed by the acceptance of the Babylonian system of vowel points, which later fell into disuse, while other elements were written in 12th century Provence."* [Wikipedia]

1105 Rabbi Shlomo Yitzhak, RASHI, dies in Troyes France.

1150 Rediscovery of Aristotle's works begins in the Western Christian world

1166-1168 Moses Maimonides while studying at what is now the University of Al-Karaouine in Fes, Morocco, composes his commentary on the *Mishnah.*

1190 Moses Maimonides's *Guide for the Perplexed* **is published in Arabic in Cairo, Egypt, and then later translated into Hebrew.**

Circa 1201- 1300 Gerona Spain School of Kabbalah

1215 The English Nobles force their reigning King to sign the *Magna Carta* limiting the power of the king.

1247 Roger Bacon begins experimental research at Oxford England.

1248 Joseph Gikatilla born in Medinaceli Castile, Spain

1250 Moses De Leon was born in Guadalajara Spain

1266-73 Thomas Aquinas's *Summa Theologica*

Circa 1280 *The Zohar* **makes its appearance from Moses De Leon**

1280 – 1293? *Sha'are Orah (Gates of Light)* **written by Joseph Gikatilla 1293: Moses de Leon's Mishkan he Eduth**

1300 Rabbi Joseph Angelet writes a commentary for the *Sha'are Orah***.**

1305 Moses De Leon dies in Arevalo Spain and Joseph Gikatilla dies in Penafiel Spain

1310-14 Dante's *Divine Comedy*

1347-51 The Plague, aka the Black Death, sweeps Europe.**1350:** Zohar manuscripts in circulation.

1400 Geoffrey Chaucer's *Canterbury Tales*

1420 Astrologer Marziano da Tortona designed a deck for Duke Flippo Maria Visconti of Milan. He includes a fifth suit of sixteen images of the Classical gods.

1429 Joan of Arc leads French forces against invading English forces.

1442 a deck of playing cards with a fifth suit called *carte da trionfi* **appears in court records in Ferrara Italy.**

1450 a 271 card deck, with the fifth suit of trumps created for the Visconti-Sforza family, the rulers of Milan, Italy.

1455 Johannes Gutenberg's Latin *Vulgate Bible* is printed with a moveable type.

1475 Abraham ben Garton in Reggio di Calabria, Italy publishes the first Hebrew edition of the Torah with commentary, using the commentary of Rashi. Every printed Hebrew edition of the *Torah* with commentary will, from this year onwards, be published with Rashi's commentary prominently placed next to the Biblical text.

1486 Picus De Mirandula publishes *Conclusiones Philosophicae, Cabalisicae Et Theologicae.* **The beginning of the Christian Cabala.**

1487 Mainz Fortune-telling Book published in Ulm provides instructions for use of the four card suit playing cards deck for divination or fortune-telling.

1492 Jews are expelled out of Spain by King Ferdinand and Columbus set sails and reaches the Americas.

1498 Leonardo da Vinci finishes the painting *the Last Supper.*

1501 Aldus Manutius, a printer, introduces his new standard format for the printed book. He creates the pocketbook, an Octavio (eight-inch tall) size book, with a title page stating the author's name, each page was numbered, and the text had an index. He also invents italic font. The first book he published in this format was Virgil's *Opera.* This format is the invention of the comparatively inexpensive handheld book. Manutius is also the first publisher of the Greek classic texts.

1504 Michelangelo completes his sculpture of *David*

1512-14 Nicholas Copernicus's in *Commentariohs,* outlines his heliocentric theory.

1516 Thomas More writes the book *Utopia.* Latin translation of the Sha'are Orah published as the Porta Lucis by Paulos / Paolo Riccio.

1517 Marin Luther posts his theses in the city of Wittenberg, Germany challenging Papal authority. This is the beginning of the Reformation and the creation of what will become known as Protestant Christianity.

1521 The official act that openly divides the Lutherans from Roman Catholic Christianity is begun with the *Edict of Worms*, which officially excommunicated Luther and all of his followers from the Catholic Church's form of Christianity.

1522 Moses ben Jacob Cordovero, born Cordovero Spain

1523 The first complete edition of the *Babylonian Talmud* was printed in Venice by Daniel Bomberg. In addition to the *Mishnah* and *Gemara*, Bomberg's edition contained the commentaries of Rashi and *Tosafot*. Henceforth every edition of the *Talmud* would follow this format and include the comprehensive commentary of Rashi.

1530 A deck with a fifth suit of trumps called *carte da trionfi* is called *a Tarocchi deck* to be played with.

1531or 1533 German Heinrich von Nettesheim aka Cornelius Agrippa (1486-1535) publishes *De Occulta Philosophia, the* next major text on Christian Cabala and Occult Qabalah.

1534 Isaac Luria (the ARI) was born in Jerusalem, Palestine. Henry the VIII of England issued the *Act of Supremacy* rejecting Papal control in England. Luther completes translation of the Latin Vulgate Christian Bible into the German language. This is the first translation of the Christian Bible into an accessible common language. This begins a long series of translations for a similar purpose, to make the text accessible to all Christian believers.

1540 the book *Le Sorti* published in Venice provides instructions on how to use ordinary four-suit playing cards for divination or fortune-telling.

1541 Michelangelo completes the *Last Judgment*

1542 Establishment of the Roman Inquisition by the Catholic Church

1542/48 Moses ben Jacob Cordovero's notes' on his study of the *Zohar* is finished: *Pardes Rimonim (Garden / Orchard of Pomegranates)*

1552 William Postell (Gulelmus Postellus 1510-1581) First translation of the Sefer Yetzirah. Latin version based on the short version of the text. Published in Paris.[2]

1555 *The Peace of Augsburg* a treaty between Charles V of the Catholic Holy Roman Empire and the forces of an alliance of Lutheran princes is signed on September 25, 1555, at the imperial city of Augsburg, now in present-day Bavaria, Germany. It officially ends the first religious war between the two groups and made the legal division of Christendom permanent within the territories controlled by the Holy Roman Empire.

1558 *The Zohar* **first published book edition**

1561 Joseph Gikatilla's *Sha' are Orah* **published**

1569 Rabbi Isaac Luria moves to Safed, Palestine.

1570 Moses ben Jacob Cordovero dies

1572 Isaac Luria dies in Safed. Chaim Vital, the disciple of Luria begins to record the teachings of Luria. Tycho Brahe records the observation of a supernova.

1584 Giordano Bruno (born in Nola Italy 1548) publishes *La Cene de le Ceneeri* (*The Ash Wednesday Supper*) and *De la Causa, Principio et Uno* (*On Cause, Principle and Unity*)

1587 John Pistor (Johannes Pistorius 1546-1608) publishes a Latin translation of the Sefer Yetzirah. 'At the end of the manuscript that is held in the British Museum, Ms. 740, there is a note that it was written in 1488 by a Jew, Yitzchak of Rome[3]**'**

1590 Dutch spectacle makers Hans Jansen and his son Zacharias Jansen, claimed by later writers Pierre Borel or William Borel, to have

---

[2] (Kaplan 1990, 336-337)
[3] (Kaplan 1990, 336)

invented a device to study small objects by looking through the compound lenses, and thus created his version of what will be called the microscope.

1590- 1607 These are the years when William Shakespeare wrote and had his first performances of his plays, such as *The Taming of the Shrew, Romeo and Juliet, The Merchant of Venice, Hamlet, A Midsummer's Night Dream,* and *Macbeth.*

1591 Moses ben Jacob Cordovero's *Pardes Rimonim* is first published

1600 Giordano Bruno was burned at the stake for heresy by the Catholic Church.

1601/02 Athanasius Kircher born in Geisa Germany

1604 Johannes Kepler *Supplement to Witelo.*

1609 Galileo Galilei develops a magnifying device to study small objects with a convex and a concave lens.

1616 Catholic Church declares Copernican theory of heliocentric solar system false and erroneous.

1618 The beginning of what will be known as the Thirty Year War; a religious war between the forces of Protestant Christian governments with the forces of the Catholic Holy Roman Empire in Europe.

1619 or 1621 Cornelius Drebbel presents in London a compound devise to study small objects with two convex lenses, his version of what will be called the microscope. **Chaim Vital dies. Chaim Vital's son, Rabbi Shmuel Vital, edited and re-arranged these copies in eight sections, known as the Shemoneh She'arim. He began circulating them in manuscript form only**

1625 Giovanni Faber coins the word microscope by analogy to the telescope for these devices that magnify small objects that Jansen, Galileo, and Drebbel had invented. **Philippe d'Aquin publishes the *Tree of Kabbalah.***

1626 Shabbatai Tzvi[4] born in Smyrna, Turkey.

1627 Before Chaim Vital died in 5380 (1620 CE) he ordered that all his manuscripts be buried with him. Several years later, after asking his permission in a kabbalistic rite known as sh'eilat chalom, Rabbi Abraham Azulai and Rabbi Yaakov Tzemach, colleagues and disciples of Rabbi Chaim, extracted the writings from Rabbi Chaim's grave and published them. This version of the Etz Chaim is known as the mehadura batra (the later version).

1632 Baruch Spinoza was born in Amsterdam, Dutch Republic.

1633 In July of that year, the inquisition concluded with Galileo being threatened with torture if he did not tell the truth, but he maintained his denial. He denied that he had ever held Copernican ideas after 1616 or ever intended to defend them in the Dialogue despite the threat of torture. The sentence of the Inquisition was delivered on 22 June. It was in three essential parts: Galileo was found "vehemently suspect of heresy", namely of having held the opinions that the Sun lies motionless at the center of the universe, that the Earth is not at its center and moves, and that one may hold and defend an opinion as probable after it has been declared contrary to Holy Scripture. He was required to "abjure, curse and detest" those opinions. He was sentenced to formal imprisonment at the pleasure of the Inquisition. On the following day, this was commuted to house arrest, which he remained   under   for   the   rest   of   his   life. [https://en.wikipedia.org/wiki/Galileo_Galilei#Controversy_over_heliocentrism]

His offending Dialogue was banned; and in an action not announced at the trial, publication of any of his works was forbidden, including any he might write in the future.[87]

1642 John Stephan Rittangel (Joanne Stephano Rittangelio 1606-1652) Publishes a Latin translation of the *Sefer Yetzirah*. It contains the

---

[4] Tzvi's life as a false Messiah caused a major catastrophe in the Jewish community and its repercussions were felt for years to come, especially in the response to the Hassidic movement in the 1700's.

Hebrew text and commentary of R. Abraham ben David (Raavad) also the Thirty-two Paths of Wisdom.[5]

1648 The end of what will be known as The Thirty Year War between Protestant Christian forces and the Catholic Christian forces of the Holy Roman Empire in Europe. Shabbatai Tzvi At age 22 in 1648, Sabbatai started declaring to his followers in Smyrna that he was the true Messianic redeemer. [For details on the life and events of Shabbatai Tzvi check out https://en.wikipedia.org/wiki/Sabbatai_Zevi]

1650 – 1654 Athanasius Kircher publishes *Oedipus Aegyptiacus.*

1653 Athanasius Kircher's text the *Oedipus Aegyptiacus*, v. 2:1 contains a translation of the *Sefer Yetzirah* in Latin.

Rabbi Meir Poppers, a disciple of Tzemach, combined both versions of Chaim Vital's Etz Chaim, the record of Luria's teachings, as well as others that were found elsewhere (apparently in Hebron and Italy) in the final edition that was completed in 5413 (1653 CE).

1665 Robert Hooke publishes *Micrographia*, a collection of biological micrographs. He coins the word cell for the structures he discovers in cork bark. Baruch Spinoza wrote *Ethics, Demonstrated in Geometrical Order (Latin: Ethica, ordine geometrico demonstrata),* usually known as the Ethics, is a philosophical treatise It was written between 1664 and 1665 and was first published in 1677. The book is perhaps the most ambitious attempt to apply the method of Euclid in philosophy. Spinoza puts forward a small number of definitions and axioms from which he attempts to derive hundreds of propositions and corollaries, such as "When the Mind imagines its own lack of power, it is saddened by it",[Part 3, proposition 33.] "A free man thinks of nothing less than of death",[Part 4, proposition 67] and "The human mind cannot be absolutely destroyed with the body, but something of it remains which is eternal."[Part 5, proposition 23]

1666 Sabbatai Tzvi was confronted by the sultan's vizier gave him three choices; subject himself to a trial of his divinity in the form of a volley of arrows (in which should the archers miss, his divinity would be proven);

---

[5] (Kaplan 1990, 337)

be impaled, or he could convert to Islam. On the following day (September 16, 1666) Tzvi came before the sultan, cast off his Jewish garb, and put a Turkish turban on his head. Thus, his conversion to Islam was accomplished.

1670 Baruch Spinoza's *Tractatus Theologico-Politicus* or *Theologico-Political Treatise* published anonymously. In the treatise, Spinoza put forth his most systematic critique of Judaism and all organized religion in general. Spinoza argued that theology and philosophy must be kept separate, particularly in the reading of scripture. Whereas the goal of theology is obedience, philosophy aims at understanding rational truth. Scripture does not teach philosophy and thus cannot be made to conform with it, otherwise, the meaning of scripture will be distorted. Conversely, if reason is made subservient to scripture, then, Spinoza argues, "the prejudices of a common people of long ago... will gain a hold on his understanding and darken it." He reinterpreted the belief that there were such things as prophecy, miracles, or supernatural occurrences. He argued that God acts solely by the laws of "his own nature". He rejected the view that God had a particular end game or purpose to advance in the course of events: to Spinoza, those who believed so were only creating a delusion for themselves out of fear.

1672 Isaac Newton publishes his first presentation of the theory of light and color in the Philosophical Transactions of the Royal Society.

1673 Anton van Leeuwenhoek improves on the process of making lenses without grinding them for his microscope. He began a major investigation of microbiology and is considered the 'father' of this study. He corresponds with the Royal Society of London concerning his work, which continues through to 1716.

1677 Baruch Spinoza dies in the Hague, Dutch Republic. Spinoza's *Ethics* was published after his death.

1684 Christian Knorr von Rosenroth's *Kabbala Denudata (The Hidden Kabbala*) published.

1687 Isaac Newton's important texts *Principia Mathematica* and *Philosophiae Naturalis* are published.

1698? Israel ben Eliezer (The Baal Shem Tov) born in Okopy, Poland

1704 Isaac Newton waits for the death of Robert Hooke, and then Newton publishes his new presentation of light in *Opticks*.

1708 Rabbi Mordecai Ben Jacob's *Pa'amon ve Rimmon (Bell and Pomegranate).*

1710 Bishop Berkeley publishes his *Principles of Human Knowledge.* **Dov Ber born in Bolhynia, he will become Rabbi Dov Ber, the Maggid of Mezeritch, and the leader of the Hassidic movement after the death of the Baal Shem Tov**

1719 First publication of ARI's commentary to the *Sefer Yetzirah*

Circa 1720 Israel ben Eliezer takes on the title Baal Shem. Elijah ben Shlomo Zalmen Kremer (the GRA) was born in Vilna Lithuania.

1724 Johan Sebastian Bach composes and preforms his *Passion According to Saint John.*

1740 Israel Ben Eliezer, takes on the title of the Baal Shem Tov, the Master of the Good Name, and begins his teachings in the small city of Medzhybizh in the Ukraine. It is his own form of Judaism, which will be known as Hassidism. David Hume publishes his *Treatise on Human Nature.*

1741 George Frideric Handel composes and preforms his *Messiah.*

1752 Benjamin Franklin demonstrates that lightning is a form of electricity.

1760 Israel ben Eliezer, The Baal Shem Tov, dies Medzhybizh, Poland and Rabbi Dov Ber of Mezeritch (the Maggid) becomes the next leader of the Hassidic movement

1770 Parisian occultist Jean-Baptiste Alliette, publishes Etteilla, or a Method of Entertaining Oneself with a pack of cards, therein he

describes his method of divination using the common four-suit deck of playing cards. He also briefly mentions the Tarot deck, those with the fifth suit of trumps as a divination tool.

1768 *Encyclopedia Britannica* is published for the first time.

April 11, 1772, the first major pronouncement of an excommunication against Hasidism was issued by the GRA. Maggid's pupils Menachem Mendel of Vitebsk and Rabbi Shneur Zalman of Liadi visit the GRA and try to bring reconciliation between the GRA's Mitnagdim and Hassidism. This fails. Rabbi Shneur Zalman founds Chabad Hassidic movement. December: Rabbi Dov Ber dies in Hanipol, Poland

1775 The American Revolution begins.

1776 Thomas Jefferson et al, drafts the *Declaration of Independence*. Adam Smith publishes his economic treatise describing the hidden hand of capitalism in the *Wealth of Nations*.

1778 Antoine Court de Gebelin's nine volumes set *Le Monde Primitif Analyse et Compare avec le Monde Moderne,* **published in Paris. His essay presents the idea that the Tarot was of Egyptian origin based on his fake 'translation' of Egyptian hieroglyphics. Gebelin invites Louis-Raphael-Lucrece de Fayolle, le Comte de Mellet to publish an essay on the Tarot as well. De Mellet begins the process of matching the Tarot's Major Arcana to be linked to the letters of the Hebrew alphabet.**

1779 Elijah ben Shlomo Zalmen Kremer (GRA) dies in Vilna, Lithuania.

1781 Immanuel Kant publishes his *Critique of Pure Reason;* he explains that it is a response to the work of David Hume, and Bishop George Berkeley.

1785 Jean-Baptiste Alliette aka Etteilla publishes *A Way to Entertain Oneself with a Pack of Cards Called Tarots.* **Etteilla repeats the Egyptian origin story of the Tarot calling the deck the book of Thoth.**

1787-88 In America, James Madison, Alexander Hamilton, and John Jay publish and distribute *The Federalist Papers*. Mozart performs his *Don Giovanni*.

1788 In July the final 11th state assembly ratifies the U. S. constitution.

1789 On March 4, 1789, the United States of America government began operations. The French Revolution begins. James Madison introduces the first ten amendments to the new constitution to the first congress of the United States of America. **Jean-Baptiste Alliette aka Etteilla publishes his first new Tarot deck specifically made for divination. He calls this deck the Book of Thoth.**

1791 The eleventh state assembly ratifies the 10 amendments, also known as *The Bill of Rights*, to the *U. S. Constitution*. These amendments have now become law.

1792 Mary Wollstonecraft publishes *Vindication of the Rights of Woman*.

1794 Mary Wollstonecraft's publishes *An Historical and Moral View of the French Revolution*.

1797 Mary Godwin was born to Mary Wollstonecraft and William Godwin.

1799 Napoleon Bonaparte becomes the first consul in France officially ending the French Revolution. French soldiers find the 'Rosetta Stone' in Egypt; it contains two forms of ancient Egyptian writings and the third section is in ancient Greek.

1803 Ludwig van Beethoven composes and performs *Eroica* Symphony no. 3.

1806 GRA's edition with his commentary of the *Sefer Yetzirah* published.

1807 G W F Hegel publishes *The Phenomenology of Spirit*.

1811-1813 Jane Austen publishes her novels *Sense and Sensibility* and *Pride and Prejudice.*

1814 Mary Godwin begins a romance with the married Percy Bysshe Shelley. In 1816 Mary and Percy become officially married and she officially becomes Mary Shelley. In the constantly cold and rainy summer of that year, the long cold weather was caused by the eruption in 1815 of Mount Tambora on the northern coast of Sumbawa island, Indonesia; they spend time with Lord Byron, John Polidori, and Mary's stepsister, Claire Clairmont, in Geneva, Switzerland at the Villa Diodati. This is when Percy, Shelley, Byron, and Polidori begin to see who can craft the best 'ghost stories for their amusement.

1818 Mary Shelley publishes her novel *Frankenstein; or, The Modern Prometheus.* The first edition was published anonymously in London. The second edition published in 1823 was published under her own name.

1822 Jean Francois Champollion announces that he has translated the Rosetta Stone and translates Egyptian hieroglyphs for the first time.

1824 Ludwig van Beethoven finishes and performs his *Symphony no. 9.*

1826 Mary Shelley publishes her third book, the apocalyptic science fiction novel, *The Last Man.*

1830 Yohann Freidrich von Meyer translates the *Sefer Yetzirah* into German.

1834 Edgar Allan Poe publishes the poem *To One in Paradise.*

1835 Alexis de Tocqueville publishes his *Democracy in America.*

1836 Ralph Waldo Emerson publishes his essay *Nature,* as part of the Transcendentalism philosophic tradition.

1837 Emerson gives the *"American Scholar"* address. Charles Dicken's publishes *Pickwick Papers.*

1838 *Oliver Twist* published by Charles Dickens

1839- 1842 Edgar Allan Poe publishes *The Fall of the House of Usher, Murder in the Rue Morgue, and Masque of the Red Death*

1843 John Stuart Mill publishes his *System of Logic*. Edgar Allan Poe publishes *The Tell Tale Heart*. Soren Kierkegaard's *Either/Or, Fear and Trembling* published.

1844 Samuel F B Morse dispatches the first telegram

1845 Michael Faraday shows through experimental evidence that both Magnets and electricity generate fields of force. He also discovers that light propagation can be influenced by external magnetic fields. Henry David Thoreau builds a cabin at Walden Pond to work on his writings and to live a simple life. Edgar Allan Poe publishes *The Purloined Letter* and *The Raven.*

1846 Michael Faraday gives a lecture at the English Royal Institution in which he proposes his view that there is unity in the forces of nature. He proposes that the field lines of electricity and magnets are associated with atoms and that this could provide the medium by which light waves were propagated without the aether. Fields of force connect the atomic particles. The vibrations of these fields create the waves of light, electricity, and magnetism. Edgar Allan Poe publishes *The Cask of Amontillado.*

1847 Hermann Von Helmholtz describes the law of the conservation of energy. Thoreau leaves Walden Pond. Charlotte Bronte publishes her novel *Jane Eyre* and Emily Bronte publishes *Wuthering Heights.*

1848 Karl Mark and Friedrich Engels write and publish *Communist Manifesto*. The Women's suffrage movement begins in the United States. Henry David Thoreau publishes '*Resistance to Civil Government*' that became known as '*Civil Disobediences*'.

1851 Herman Melville publishes *Moby Dick*

1854 Eliphas Levi's first book *Dogma et Rituel de la Haute Magie: The Dogma and Rituals of High Magic* was published. Levi fleshes out the

idea that the Major Arcana is matched to the Hebrew alphabet. Henry David Thoreau publishes *Walden*.

1855 Walt Whitman publishes the first edition of *Leaves of Grass*

1859 Charles Darwin publishes *The Origin of Species*. John Stuart Mill publishes *On Liberty*. Charles Dickens publishes *A Tale of Two Cities*.

1860 Robert Bunsen and Gustav Kirchhoff observe dark lines in the spectrum of a light source pass through burning substances.

1861 Within the United States of America the Civil War begins. James Clark Maxwell, using Thomas Young's theory of color and vision, produces the first color photographic image. **Eliphas Levi *publishes La Clef des Grands Mysteres*.**

1862 James Clark Maxwell realizes that electricity and magnetism have to be related to light when he discovers that they all traveled at the same speed. Maxwell uses Robert Faraday's ideas and works to build a mathematical theory of the unified field of magnets and electricity. Victor Hugo Publishes *Les Miserables*.

1863 The *Emancipation Proclamation* is issued. Abraham Lincoln gives his *Gettysburg Address*. **The manuscript of Chaim Vital's recording of his master Isaac Luria's teaching was eventually printed in seven volumes in Jerusalem 5623-5658 (1863-98 CE) with the support of the kabbalists of the Bet-El Yeshiva. Many kabbalists are of the opinion that this version, known as the mehadura kamma (the first version) is the most reliable version of Rabbi Chaim's writings[6].**

1864 Jules Verne publishes his novel *Journey to the Center of the Earth*. Louis Pasteur completes the first successful experiment of the procedure to be known as pasteurization.

---

[6]   Source:
http://www.chabad.org/kabbalah/article_cdo/aid/380689/jewish/Works-of-Rabbi-Chaim-Vital.htm

1865 Greggor Mendel proposes his theory of genetic inheritance. Jules Verne publishes his novel *From Earth to the Moon*. President Abraham Lincoln was assassinated. **Christian David Ginsburg (a Jewish convert at age 15 to Christianity) publishes** *The Kabbalah: Its Doctrines, Development and Literature, An Essay.*

1866 Fyodor Dostoevsky's *Crime and Punishment*

1867 Karl Marx publishes *Das Kapital.*

1868 John Chalmers publishes the first complete English translation of the *Tao Te Ching*. **Frieherr Albert von Thimus translates the** *Sefer Yetzirah* **into German.**

1869 Russian Chemist Dmitry Mendeleyev, using the work of John Dalton and others, first charts the elements and organizes them in order of their atomic weights, thus establishing the *Periodic Table of Elements*. Leo Tolstoy publishes *War and Peace.*

1870 Jules Verne publishes his novel *Twenty Thousand Leagues Under the Sea.*

1871 Charles Darwin publishes *The Descent of Man.*

1872 Fredrick Nietzsche's publishes *The Birth of Tragedy*

1873 James Clark Maxwell publishes his paper *Electricity and Magnetism.*

1875 Mark Twain publishes *The Adventures of Tom Sawyer*. Helena Blavatsky forms the Theosophical Society.

1876 Alexander Graham Bell invents the telephone

1877 Alexander Graham Bell invents the phonograph. Charles Sanders Peirce publishes "The Fixation of Belief".**Isidor Kalish translates the** *Sefer Yetzirah* **into English with preface, explanatory notes, and glossary.**

1878 Charles Sanders Peirce publishes "How to Make Our Ideas Clear", this article with his previous 1877 article, lays the foundation of the system that will be known as pragmatism.

1879 Thomas Edison invents electric carbon-filament light. Henrik Ibsen's publishes *A Doll's House*.

1880 Fyodor Dostoevsky's publishes *The Brothers Karamazov*

1881 First wave of Jewish immigration to Palestine.

1884 The GRA's *Sefer Yetzirah* Warsaw edition published. Fredrick Nietzsche's *Thus Spoke Zarathustra*[7]. Twain's *Huckleberry Finn*. **Alfred Edersheim publishes an English translation of the *Sefer Yetzirah* in his book *The Life and Times of Jesus*.**

1886 Friedrich Nietzsche's *Beyond Good and Evil*

1887 S. L. MacGregor Mather publishes *The Kabbalah Unveiled*, which is an English translation of a portion of Rosenroth's *Kabbala Denudata*. Arthur Conan Doyle publishes *The Study in Scarlet*. Michelson-Morley Experiment disproves the existence of Aether. **William Wynn Westcott translates the Sefer Yetzirah into English based on the Rittangel Latin text.**

1888 William Wynn Westcott together with Samuel Liddell MacGregor Mathers founded the Hermetic Order of the Golden Dawn. Jack the Ripper murders occurred in Whitechapel London England. **Papus (Gerard Encauses) translates the *Sefer Yetzirah* into French.**

1889 The next Tarot deck to be invented for Occult divination was by Oswald Wirth. Gerard Encauses writes under the name, Gerard Encauses aka Papus, and he used Wirth's deck in his own book *Le Tarot*

---

[7] Mentioned in this book is the most famous reference to Nietzche's concept of the 'ubermench' often translated as the 'superman'. Also in this book is presented the 'death of God' idea.

des Bohemiens. **He also designs a Tarot deck.** Vincent Van Goh's Starry Night

1890 Oscar Wilde publishes *The Pictures of Dorian Gray.* William James's *Principles of Psychology* is finished after being started 12 years prior. James Frazer's *The Golden Bough.*

1891 Arthur Conan Doyle publishes *The Adventures of Sherlock Holmes,* James Legge's translation of the *Tao Te Ching.* **Meyer Lambert translates the *Sefer Yetzirah* into French.**

1892 Pyotr Ilyich Tchaikovsky performs *The Nutcracker Suite.* William James publishes *Psychology: The Briefer Course.*

1893 William Wynn Westcott's English translation of the *Sefer Yetzirah* reprinted with additional notes.

1894 Phineas Mordel translates the Sefer Yetzirah into English with the Hebrew text. '...translation in a new version deduced logically by the author, but not accepted in Kabbalistic or scholarly circles.[8]' Lazarus (Eliezer) Goldschmidt translates the *Sefer Yetzirah* into German. 'With introduction, bibliography, and notes. Hebrew texts compare all printed editions. A valuable reference work.[9]'

1895 Herbert George Wells publishes *The Time Machine.* Oscar Wilde's *The Importance of Being Earnest.*

1896 Theodore Herzl publishes *The Jewish State,* and with it creates the concept of the Zionist movement within Judaism. Anton Chekhov's *The Seagull.* Henri Becquerel discovers radioactivity in uranium.

1897 William James's *The Will to Believe and other essays.*

1898 Herbert George Wells publishes *The War of the Worlds.*

---

[8] (Kaplan 1990, 335)
[9] (Kaplan 1990, 336)

1899 William James published *Talks to Teachers on Psychology and to Students on Some of Life's Ideas.*

1900 Sigmund Freud *The Interpretation of Dreams.* Max Planck initiates quantum physics. Rediscovery of Mendelian genetics.

1901 Sylv Karppe translates *Sefer Yetzirah* into French.

1902 William James published his Gifford lectures as *The Varieties of Religious Experience.*

1903 Oliver and Wilbur Wright have the first successful airplane flight. Jack London publishes *The Call of the Wild.* George Bernard Shaw's *Man and Superman.*

1904 In a burst of inspiration Aleister Crowley transcribes his book Liber Al vel Legis, sub figura CCXX, The Book of the Law.

1905 The Russian Revolution begins. Albert Einstein publishes his Theory of Special Relativity, photoelectric effect, and Brownian motion. Sigmund Freud's *Three Essays on the Theory of Sexuality.* Máx Weber's The *Protestant Ethic and the Spirit of Capitalism.*

1906 Mahatma Gandhi develops the philosophy of nonviolent activism.

1907 William James's *Pragmatism: A New Name for Some Old Ways of Thinking,* a collection of some earlier essays plus new material. Daisetsu Teitaro Suzuki's *Outline of Mahayana Buddhism* introduces Buddhism to the West.

1909 Aleister Crowley's *Liber 777.* Arthur Edward Waite and Pamela Colman Smith publish their Tarot deck with the William Rider and Son of London publishing company. The National Association for the Advancement of Colored People was founded in the United States. William James publishes *The Meaning of Truth: A Sequel to Pragmatism* and his Hibbert lectures were published as *A Pluralistic Universe.*

1910 Arthur Edward Waite's book *The Pictorial Key to the Tarot* **was published using the drawings of his collaborator Pamela Coleman Smith.** Bertrand Russell and Alfred North Whitehead begin work on *Principia Mathematica*. William James dies on August 26.

1911 William James's incomplete manuscript published: *Some Problems of Philosophy: A Beginning of an Introduction to Philosophy*.

1912 Aleister Crowley begins his first set of commentaries to his *Book of Law.* The HMS Titanic sinks. Carl Jung publishes *Psychology of the Unconscious*. Wegner proposes the theory of continental drift. William James *Essays in Radical Empiricism* published. **Phineas Mordel reprints his 1894 translation of the** *Sefer Yetzirah* **into English, 'introduction contains important historical data and quotes significant manuscripts' in the Jewish Quarterly Review ...1912 & 1913 [finishes.] Published separately 1914.**[10]

1913 Aleister Crowley translated and published Eliphas Levi's *The Key to the Great Mysteries* **in** *Equinox* **volume Ten in the fall.** Igor Stravinsky's *Rite of Spring*. D. H. Lawrence *Sons and Lovers*. Henry Ford begins mass production of the automobile in the U.S. **E. Bischof translates the** *Sefer Yetzirah* **into German. Comtesse Calomira de Cimara translates** *Sefer Yetzirah* **into French.**

1914 The Archduke of Austria was assassinated in Serbia and is the spark that sets off World War I. Franz Kafka's *The Trial*. James Joyce's *Portrait of the Artist as a Young Man*.

1915 Albert Einstein publishes *The Theory of General Relativity*.

1917 Rudolf Otto's *The Idea of the Holy*. Beginning of the Russian Revolution.

1918 Oswald Spengler's *The Decline of the West*

---

[10] (Kaplan 1990, 335)

1919 World War I ends and the formation of the League of Nations. Hermann Hesse's *Demian*, James Watson's *Psychology from the Standpoint of a Behaviorist*.

1920 Paul Foster Case's *An Introduction to the Study of the Tarot*. October: Agatha Christie's first novel, *The Mysterious Affair at Styles*, is published in the United States, introducing the long-running Belgian detective character, Hercule Poirot, in an English country house setting. November 9 – D. H. Lawrence's novel *Women in Love* is first published, in a limited subscribers' edition in the United States. Sigmund Freud *Beyond the Pleasure Principle* published. H. G. Wells *The Outline of History* published. William Butler Yeat's *"The Second Coming"*.

1921 Crowley completes his commentary on his *Book of Law*. *The Age of Innocence* by Edith Wharton. H. Rider Haggard *She and Allan* published.

1922 *Ulysses* by James Joyce is first published complete in book form by Sylvia Beach's Shakespeare and Company in Paris on February 2 (Joyce's 40th birthday), with a further edition published in Paris for the Egoist Press of London on October 12 (much of which is seized by the United States Customs Service). T. S. Eliot founds The Criterion magazine (October) containing the first publication of his poem *The Waste Land*. This is first published complete in book form by Boni & Liveright in New York in December. Hermann Hesse's *Siddhartha*, F. Scott Fitzgerald's short story *"The Curious Case of Benjamin Button"* is published in The Smart Set magazine. Ludwig Wittgenstein *Tractatus Logico-Philosophicus* published.

1923 Charles Stansfeld Jones aka Frater Achad's *Q.B.L. or The Bride's Reception*. *The Voyages of Doctor Doolittle* by Hugh Lofting was published. Dorothy L. Sayers' *Whose Body?* (Introduces Lord Peter Wimsey, U.S. publication precedes the U.K.) T. E. Lawrence - *Seven Pillars of Wisdom* (private edition) published. P. G. Wodehouse: *The Inimitable Jeeves* published. Sigmund Freud - *The Ego and the Id* published. Khalil Gibran - *The Prophet* published. Martin Buber's *I and Thou*. Ivan Pavlov's *Conditional Reflexes*. Jean Piaget's *Language and Thought of a Child*, **S. Savini translates the *Sefer Yetzirah* into Italian. Knut Senring translates *Sefer Yetzirah* into English, with an introduction by Arthur Edward Waite.**

1924 Arthur Edward Waite's *The Holy Kabbalah: A Study of the Secret Tradition in Israel.* E. M. Forster - *A Passage to India* published. Thomas Mann - *The Magic Mountain* published. A. A. Milne - *When We Were Very Young* published. Jean Piaget's *Judgment and Reasoning in the Child.*

1925 Adolf Hitler published his autobiographical book *Mein Kampf* or *My Struggle.* A. N. Whitehead's *Science and the Modern World.* James Dewey's *Experience and Nature*

1926 Erwin Schrodinger develops wave equation underlying quantum mechanics. Jean Piaget's *Childs Conception of the World,* A. A. Milne's *Winnie the Pooh.*

1927 Paul Foster Case published *A Brief Analysis of the Tarot.* Werner Heisenberg formulates the Principle of Uncertainty. Niels Bohr formulates the Principle of Complementarity. Martin Heidegger's *Being and Time.* Sigmund Freud's *The Future of Illusion.* Hermann Hesse's *Der Steppenwolf,* Jean Piaget's *Childs Conception of Physical Causality,* D. T. Suzuki's *Essays in Zen Buddhism: First Series.*

1928 Rudolf Carnap's *The Logical Structure of the World.* Carl Jung's *The Spiritual Problem of Modern World,* A. A. Milne's *House on Pooh Corner.*

1929 A. N. Whitehead's *Process and Reality.* William Faulkner's *The Sound and the Fury.* Virginia Woolf's *A Room of One's Own.*

1930 S. Freud's *Civilization and Its Discontents.* Jose Ortega y Gasset's The *Revolt of the Masses.* Rudolf Bultmann's *The Historicity of Man and Faith*

1931 Paul Foster Case published *Highlights of Tarot.* Kurt Godel's Theorem proves the decidability of propositions in formalized mathematical systems.

1932 Israel Regardie's *A Garden of Pomegranates* **and** *The Tree of Life: A Study in Magic.* Carl Jasper's *Philosophie,* Jean Piaget's *Moral Judgment of a Child.*

1933 Adolf Hitler comes to power in Germany

1934 Arnold Toynbee's *A Study of History*. Karl Popper's *Logic of Scientific Discovery*. C. Jung's *Archetypes of the Collective Unconscious*. D.T. Suzuki's *An Introduction to Zen Buddhism* (Republished in 1948.)

1935 Dion Fortune's *The Mystical Qabalah*, and D. T. Suzuki's *Manual of Zen Buddhism*.

1936 Arthur Oncken Lovejoy's *Great Chain of Being*. Alfred Jules Ayer's *Language, Truth and Logic*. John Maynard Keynes's *General Theory of Employment, Interest and Money*, Jean-Paul Sartre's *Imagination*.

1937 Anna Freud's *The Ego and the Mechanics of Defense*. Alan Mathison Turing's *On Computable Numbers*. Jean-Paul Sartre's *Transcendence of the Ego*.

1938 Aleister Crowley begins work on his own Tarot deck. Bertolt Brecht's play *Galileo*. Discovery of nuclear fission. Jean-Paul Sartre's *Nausea*.

1939 World War II Begins and the Nazi's Final Solution is implemented aka the Holocaust.

1941 Reinhold Niebuhr's *The Nature and Destiny of Man*. Erich Fromm's *Escape from Freedom*.

1942 Albert Camus's *The Stranger* and *The Myth of Sisyphus*

1943 Crowley completes his Tarot deck. Sartre *Being and Nothingness*. Thomas Stearns Elliot's poem *Four Quartets*. H. Hesse's *The Glass Bead Game* aka *Magister Ludi*.

1944 Crowley published his Tarot deck in private circulation as *The Book of Thoth*.

1945 Jean-Paul Sartre's *The Age of Reason*, George Orwell's *Animal Farm*, E. B. White's *Stuart Little*, John Steinbeck's *Cannery Row*, Bertrand Russell's *History of Western Civilization*, Astrid Lindgren's *Pippi Longstockings*, A. E. Van Vogt's *World of Null-A*, H. P. Lovecraft's *Lurker at the Threshold* and *The Dunwich Horror*. **August 6 at 8:15 am Atomic bombs**

dropped on the Japanese cities of Hiroshima and Nagasaki by the United States of America.

2014 G M Jaron publishes *Qabalah Gates of Light*

2018 G M Jaron revises *Qabalah Gates of Light* and publishes *Qabalah Paths of Light.*

Introduction

This book is continuing the task of reconstructing the Occult Qabalah that was begun in my previous book *The Qabalah Gates of Light.* The concept of reconstruction comes out of the Neo-pagan movement as an approach to the material of a given cultural tradition. The goal of the reconstruction movement is to create a variant of the ancient culture's religious practices that can be lived in the context of today's world. It is based on an attitude of respect to the ancestors and willingness to learn from them, through the work of the scholars in the fields of archeology, anthropology, and such. To take those materials, and any work done with the recovered ancient texts, analyze them to begin to find a way to utilize them as guides in how to interact with that tradition's ideas of the sacred.

The polar opposite of the respectful acknowledgment of the ancestors is to do what Christianity has done with all indigenous cultures. Christianity co-opted their symbols and holidays or denigrated their beliefs by associating them with demonic worship. It is a fact that the Occult Qabalah, for one example of many, inadvertently, and I believe unknowingly, accepts the system of a Jesuit priest Athanasius Kircher and utilizes it as their means to understand the Kabbalah of the Jewish people.

This is disrespectful and should not be tolerated. Therefore, I will purge out of my discussion and treatment any Christian imagery, symbols and or metaphors. This means, for example, that the idea of the Fall, the idea of Original Sin, the idea of the requirement of a savior, the reference to 'the Father, Son, and the Holy Ghost, all references to Jesus, all references to a dying and resurrecting deity, all references to a mother of god, all references to the text of the 'New Testament', any references to the anti-Christ, etc. all of those ideas are foreign to a Rabbinic understanding of the Sefiroth and will be ignored and removed.

As I noted in *The Qabalah Gates of Light*, the current non-reconstructed Occult Qabalah is built upon the work and desires of the Jesuit priest Athanasius Kircher who in 1623 published his *Oedipus Aegyptiacus*, which is the source text for the Occult Qabalah[11]. I believe Kircher was motivated in a desire to eliminate the importance of the Jewish Rabbis work on the creation of the Kabbalah. Kircher used the mythic lie that eliminate the origin of the material away from the Jewish people and had it as

---

[11] Kircher falsely presents his text as being written based on the translation of Egyptian writings. This is a complete lie. No one had been able to translate Egyptian writing until the discovery of the Rosetta stone in 1799 and until Jean-François Champollion in 1822 was able to make the translations.

something transmitted to Adam and through him to the entire world's people. His use of the Rabbinic Midrashic story was intended to rob the Jews of any significant contribution. In fact, the Kabbalah is the creation of the Jewish people responding to their interaction with the Sacred as their culture perceived it. It was transmitted in Hebrew and Hebraic Aramaic, which was the exclusive language of the Hebrew / Jewish people. The material was intended to be studied exclusively by the Rabbis.

Kircher's Sefiroth, his Tree of Life, purposely ignores the logic of the source texts of the Jewish Kabbalah and thus creates the errors found in the Occult Qabalah.

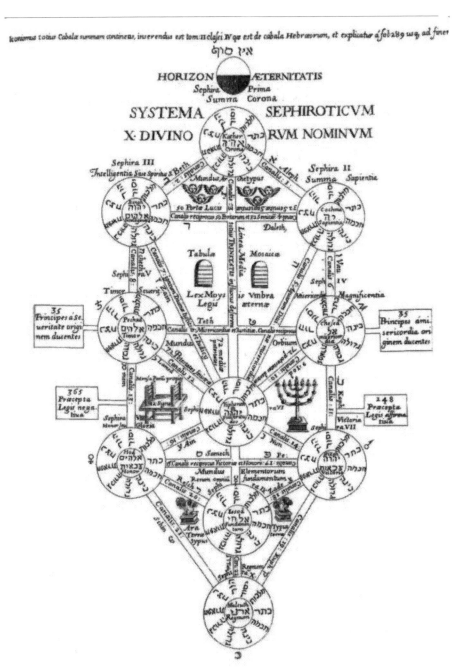

Figure 1: The Tree of Life, an engraving by Athanasius Kircher, published in his Œdipus Ægyptiacus circa 1652

I assume that the Christians who picked up the material never even noticed Kircher's intent and his results; since they grew up in a cultural environment that didn't consider the Jews to be important and believed that their own Christianized Western culture was the culmination of development on the planet.

It is as if the Jesuit Kircher ripped the Jewish Tree out of its cultural environment and therefore killed it and then locked it away in a display case to be used. That is how Christian Cabala was born and from that action, the Occult Qabalah was subsequently created.

This error could have been avoided many times down through the years. As I noted in my chronology, the *Sefer Yetzirah* was available in Latin, French, German, and English for many years, important members of the Golden Dawn, William Wynn Westcott in 1893, for example, did a translation into English. Yet no Qabalah scholar that I have come across had worked to correct the glaring errors in Kircher's tree. For example, in 1999 Chic Cicero and Sandra Tabatha Cicero published a new edited and annotated edition of a text originally by Israel Regardie, *A Garden of Pomegranates: Skrying on the Tree of Life*[12]. In this book the *Sefer Yetzirah*,

---

[12] (Cicero and Cicero 1999)

according to their index, is mentioned, referenced, and discussed 36

separate times[13]. Yet they still use the Tree with the Hebrew letters assigned

to the paths as created by Kircher[14]. Compare the two Trees and you can see

how the placements are identical.

---

[13] (Cicero and Cicero 1999, 517)
[14] (Cicero and Cicero 1999, 67)

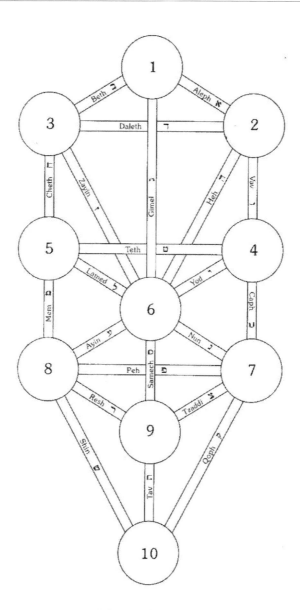

Figure 7: The Paths

Figure 2: From Cicero & Cicero's: A Garden of Pomegranates

In 2001 Lon Milo Duquette publishes *The Chicken Qabalah of Rabbi Lamed Ben Clifford: A Dilettante's Guide to What You Do and Do Not Need to Know to Become a Qabalist. (A NEW IMPROVED QABALISTIC TEXT OF GREAT CYNICISM AND WISDOM WRITTEN EXPRESSLY FOR DILETTANTES WITH REALLY SHORT ATTENTION SPANS WHO PRETENTIOUSLY CONSIDER THEMSELVES HERMETIC QABALISTS BUT WHO ARE NONETHELESS SERIOUS ABOUT UTILIZING A TINY PORTION OF THE HEBREW QABALAH FOR SPIRITUAL ENLIGHTENMENT).*[15] On pp 25-36 he discusses and offers a translation of the *Sefer Yetzirah* in English. On pp 37-67 he offers his insights and knowledge on the Hebrew letters and how they apply to the paths of the Tree. Figure 8 on pg. 44 of his book shows the Tree with those Hebrew letters assigned.

---

[15] (Duquette 2001)

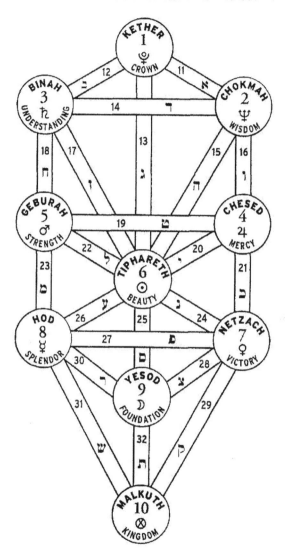

Figure 8. The Tree of Life.

Figure 3: Chicken Kabbalah's Tree p. 43.

Notice the placement. It should look familiar. You have just seen it in the previous two figures. Duquette, when it comes to understanding the Hebrew letters on the Tree, offers you nothing in the way of new insights. He just serves up the same misinformation that has been handed down within the Occult Qabalistic community since the time of that Jesuit Priest Kircher in 1653.

To my knowledge, this book you are holding is the only one that begins to actually try to understand what is going on with the *Sefer Yetzirah* and the correct and obvious, to me anyway, assignment of the Hebrew letters to the Sefirot, the Tree of Life.

I want to return the Tree of Life and Knowledge, the Sefiroth, back to its cultural roots and environment, to give it the life and purpose it once had. In doing this I will be able to offer a reconstructed Qabalah system to work with.

My project has been to bypass Kircher and instead, to go back to the actual source material of the Rabbis. We can do this since many useful rabbinic texts have been translated into English from the 1980's onward.

By examining the *Sefer Yetzirah* we can see that the key to understanding the Sefiroth is the 3, 7, 12 patterns of the Hebrew letters and the paths on the Tree. This pattern in the *Sefer Yetzirah* is what I will use to re-align the letters to the paths in a new way. In my 2014 edition of my

Qabalah Gates of Light, I offered a Tree with Hebrew letters assigned to it that

is different from the one I am suggesting now. This goes to show that there

are many maps of the Territory, each with its own context and reasoning. I

have decided that the map used in the 2014 edition is not the one I will

continue to work with. Ultimately I will now suggest using a variation based

on the GRA's 1884 pattern.

The GRA is the name given to the Gaon (the genius) Rabbi Elijahu

of Vilna Lithuania who lived during 1720-1797. It was from his work on the

Sefer Yetzirah, that I will take the pattern of the Hebrew letters that we follow

for this array structure.

GRA's array was built upon the array first presented by Rabbi

Joseph Gikatilla in his text *Sha'are Orah,* The Gates of Light. That book was

written around 1290 and it was translated into Latin by Paulus Riccius, a

convert from Judaism to Christianity, and published in book form in 1516.

The array that was used by Rabbi Gikatilla was also used by the Zohar and

eventually Rabbi Isaac Luria.

In contrast, the placement of the letters onto the paths as presented

by ARI, Rabbi Isaac Luria, is based on a very specific insight that he had.

Luria's tree and the logic used to place the letters are not easily discernible and therefore not readably accessible. Hence not the system that I will be referring to in this book.

I will use the GRA's system of letter placement whose logic is transparent and easy to understand. I will make use of the diagram presented in Aryeh Kaplan's *Sefer Yetzirah* the revised 1997 edition. The diagram is shown on the cover of that edition and on page 31 of the text as Figure 6. The description accompanying the image states: '*The paths defined by the GRA, as they appear in the Warsaw, 1884 edition. (p. 26b of Part Two).*'

Now Kaplan offers Figure 5 which he calls '*The 32 paths according to the Gra*'[16]. This array does not match up with the array as presented in Figure 6 which is the GRA's actual work. I consider Figure 5 to be the creation of Kaplan and I will not use it[17]. It is a form of the Tree that Kaplan states: '*In practice, for reasons dealing with the basic nature of the Sefiroth, they are not arranged in this natural order…*[18]' The array of Figure 5 is Kaplan's 'natural order'. We will follow the Kabbalah's tradition as it was worked out and not use that array and its letter placement that Kaplan concocted.

---

[16] (Kaplan 1990, 30)

[17] I will explain this in a latter chapter.

[18] (Kaplan 1990, 32)

Additionally, I will be offering my own theological insights throughout this book. My ideas are based on my readings of rabbinic literature in the primary source that have been translated into English and on secondary sources. I take the trends that I see in that literature and go further along paths of my choosing.

The Rabbis created Oral Torah, the idea that the written sacred text cannot be truly understood without the addition of commentaries and addendums, which were first passed down orally and later became themselves written down, although they retained the overall label of 'oral tradition'. This Oral Torah is a vast ocean, to use one metaphor from the Rabbis, or a huge tapestry, to offer another metaphor. Within that vast, colorful, and diverse tapestry are many different strands. My own work follows and emphasizes a selection of those strands and deemphasizes or ignores others. This is part of the 'game of the rabbis' who created the ongoing oral tradition.

For instance, the Hebrews literally invented the concept of the scapegoat and developed it as a metaphor for their theology[19]. This scapegoat metaphor travels through the Biblical text and continues on into

---

[19] Leviticus 16

the writings of the rabbis. What I mean by the scapegoat metaphor is the default world view which explains that any significant issue of pain or suffering that is experienced collectively by humanity or the Hebrew-Judeans-Jewish people is not an accident. It is the fault of someone in the past who is the cause for the present misery. That persons, or groups of people, are the scapegoat. Heaped upon them is the blame for the current sufferings. This association of blame goes back to Adam and/or Eve and is a continual theme in Biblical and Rabbinic literature.

Within the Christian Cabala, and within the Occult Qabalah, there is a similar blaming metaphor, though theirs are more wrapped up in a sense of inevitable and deterministic fate and destiny. This is the idea of the Fall, of original sin and the absolute need for an intervening divine savior. All of that is the invention of Christianity and it is not a part of the Hebrews, Judeans, or the Rabbi's thinking. Within the Hebrew-Judean-Rabbinic, tradition is the optimistic belief in the potential for human rights action. This strand contains the belief that we can make things right, it is just countered with the recognition that things aren't right. Hence the need to explain and blame someone for the current mess.

My theology recognizes that things are not right, and utilizes the idea that we have the power to make things better. Though the past shape the environment that we grew up in, it does not determine our fate or destiny. We all have the potential, and for most, an ongoing opportunity to makes things better. Acts of Tikkun are ever-present for those who listen and observe. I will, therefore, offer mythology and theology that builds upon those themes.

Another aspect of the Rabbi's thinking is the willingness to incorporate the best of other culture's thinker's ideas and beliefs. They were eager to take the genius of others and incorporate it into their own work; which is why Platonic, Aristotelian, and Neo-Platonic ideas were adopted by the Rabbis. Although, I take issue with the strict rigidity of Aristotelian logic, the black and white exclusivity. I believe that the three laws of Aristotelian thinking are simply one modality of logic and the one suited to understand and work with physical concrete objects and phenomena. Whereas to deal with abstractions you need to apply seemingly contradictory logic and the middle ground. This is why I utilize the works of Lao Tzu's *The Tao Te Ching*[20] and the concepts from Alfred Korzybski[21]

---

[20] I specifically find the translation and writings of Ellen M. Chen are particularly insightful. Her 1989 new translation with commentary published by Paragon House and *In Praise of Nothing: An Exploration of Daoist Fundamental Ontology*, 2011, Xlibris.

[21] Alfred Korzybski, *Science and Sanity: An Introduction to Non-Aristotelian Systems and General Semantics*, original copyright 1933.

An important concept inspired by Korzybski I need to mention now. It is the relationship between maps and the Territory. The Territory is the infinite all, the total data of the events and interactions from the Big Bang to the present. The Territory is a non-symbolic data set. It is directly experienced non-symbolically and thus non-verbally. What we do in attempting to understand anything and everything is to select a finite subset of the available data in order to create and comprehend meaningful relationships. This process is called map making. Each map is a finite set of data that is organized with some structural purpose. There is no end to map-making since you need an infinite number of maps to equal the infinite amount of data that is the Territory.

Therefore every human idea and concept is a map. The mapmaker is shaped by her nature, her nurture, her culture, and her experience. These set out the limits and the basis for someone's map-making. The Rabbis collected, made use of, and themselves made many maps. They had only a finite set of data and experiences to draw upon. Hence their Platonic, Aristotelian, and Neo-Platonic inspired maps are not all that is needed to understand the infinite that is the Territory, or as the Jewish mystics would call it, Ayn Sof. Hence my utilizing Lao Tzu's Taoism is just making use of another set of maps to understand the Territory/Ayn Sof. My theological concepts are just another set of maps that are available to be used to help us to find our way.

This book will also explore the Occult Qabalah's understanding of the paths of the Sefiroth using my new reconstructed systems. This, of course, means that we will explore the connections made between the paths and the Major Arcana of the Tarot. Even though there is no such connection in the Jewish Kabbalah to the Tarot, it is a brilliant and original connection of the historical Occult Qabalah. This was first offered up by Le Comte de Mellet in 1782, with the full match of the letters to the Major Arcana being finally done by Eliphas Levi in 1854.

Differences Between this Book and My Gates of Light

In the first edition of my first book *The Qabalah Gates of Light*, I had made some mistakes based on inaccurate assumptions.

My first mistaken assumption was to consider that Kaplan's 'Natural Array' was actually the Tree as the GRA conceived it. In the First edition, on page 80 of the *Qabalah Gates of Light*, I state that *'Rabbi Elijah the Gaon...choose this natural array configuration for his work on the Sefer Yetzirah, and his text was first published in 1806. (See Figure 1).'* That was a mistake. The GRA's Tree was not Kaplan's Natural Array. The GRA's Tree appears to be the array used in the 1884 text of the *Sefer Yetzirah*. (See pages 115 and 156 of this book.)

The next difference between this book and my first is concerning my assignment of the Hebrew letters to the Tree. *'Figure 9 is the Enclosed Tree with my assignment of the GRA Letters onto it.'* (Jaron, 2014, 115) If you compare those letter assignments and my comments in this book you will realize they are based on two different ideas. I made some assumptions in my prior analysis that I now realize give us a possibly valid assignment of the letters based on the 3-7-12 pattern but it is an inaccurate interpretation of the GRA's 1884 Tree.

The point being, that if at any time those Occult Qabalists had attempted to follow the 3-7-12 pattern from the *Sefer Yetzirah*, whose translation was available to them and had they rejected Kircher's nonsensical assignment in the process, then we would have had a Qabalah Tree that could have been passed down to us, and we would and could have used. If that had been done, then the two traditions would not have been so far out of alignment. However, this did not happen.

I offer my assignment of the GRA's letters to the Zohar/ARI tree as something to use going forward in a Qabalah working and understanding of the Sefiroth. I hope you will use my system. It follows an actual Rabbi's assignment of the letters and one that is easily understood as derived from the 3-7-12 pattern as described in the *Sefer Yetzirah*.

Obviously, there are potentially as many maps of the Territory as there are mapmakers. So you could devise your own letter assignment. However, for the sake of consistency and commonality within the Qabalah tradition going forward, it would be of great assistance for common understanding and communication, if we all used a similar map of the Territory, hence I hope that you will use the letter assignments that I offer in this book.

Why embrace a different Tree?

I know that what I'm asking is significant. Many of you, students of the Occult Qabalah, have been working with the existing Tree and its correspondences for many years. There is the adage, 'Why fix what isn't broken?' Why change to something new and untried when the existing system has served so many for so long?

The problem is that the existing Tree is based on the Christian mythos. It is soaked in the notion of Original Sin, the metaphor of the 'Fallen Tree', the disruption of the connection of the Divine and humanity, all of that calls for the need for outside intervention and the helplessness of humanity.

I wish to replace all of that with the mythos and ethos of a variant of Rabbinic Judaism and the Kabalistic traditions that flow from the teachings of Rabbi Isaac Luria, the ARI.

(What follows next is filled with 'spoilers' or hints at what is to come when I fully present the stories of Creation according to the ideas of ARI.)

With Christianity humanity is trapped in sin and damnation and requires a savior. According to my reading of the mythology of ARI, it is

God who needs saving and we were created to be the saviors of the Divine and the cosmos.

I am hoping that you became involved in the Occult out of a desire to leave Christianity behind. You were unsatisfied with its teachings and you desired something else.

Hence I am appealing to you, to completely leave that tainted teachings, rid yourself of the last hidden remnants of its theology of despair and sin that lurks in the Occult Qabalah through the creation of the Jesuit priest Kircher who is the source of the Occult Tree. Replace that system with a new ethos and mythos. One of hope.

Each one of us is unique in the cosmos. We will exist only once in our current configuration and personal history. Thus we are all the most precious and irreplaceable things in all of the history of the cosmos. The current incarnation of our life history will never be duplicated in the vast history of the cosmos. Therefore through our uniqueness, we can uniquely contribute to Tikkun Olam, the healing of the cosmos by our individual differences.

Throughout our lives, there come moments when each one of us may find ourselves in a situation where you, and you alone, can act to help another. Hence by our actions, another person is helped and you are helped as well, additionally, the cosmic harmony is enhanced.

Every act of kindness, goodness, beauty, truth, and justice brings about the restoration of healing and harmony to the cosmos and to the Divine. This is the message of the Rabbinic Kabbalah and its Tree of Life and Knowledge. This is the message of ARI's mythos.

By leaving behind the old system and taking up this new one, you can contribute to the healing of the cosmos, the restoration of harmony. Won't you hear the song of Tikkun Olam that the Divine is singing out? Leave behind the old system and embrace this one, for the sake of the cosmos, the Divine, and ultimately, yourself.

Embracing the Tao as Ayn Sof

I wish to abandon the Neo-Platonic and Aristotelian influences behind the concept and meaning of Ayn Sof and the Rabbinic Kabbalah as a whole. I wish to replace it with the Daoist system as I understand it from the writings of Ellen M. Chen. Specifically drawing from her book *In Praise of Nothing: An Exploration of Daoist Fundamental Ontology.*

So, what does this mean? Let me quote from Chen:

1. *Greek philosophy begins with the divine as the primordial ground. Anaximander's Apeiron (Infinite) is the time deity that swallows her children. Rebellion of the children begins here.*
2. *The dethroning of the Apeiron, which becomes the Void: repudiation of Time and identity of ousia (being) with form, the Pythagoreans.*
3. *The invention of space and immobility: Xenophanes, Parmenides, and the Pluralists.*
4. *Plato's divine duality (soul and form) and battle of giants (materialists) and gods (friends of forms), forms as philosophical equivalents of gods in Olympian pantheon, the Demiurgus (World Soul) as Creator, the Void as matter, as restlessness.*
5. *For Aristotle, form is actuality prior to matter as potentiality. Aristotle's God, separable and a "this", is the Unmoved Mover, the most successful example of the flight from death. …In the Western metaphysical tradition, the immortal is understood to be what can exist apart from matter, change, and body, hence the story of early Western metaphysics as the flight from death. (Chen, 66-67)*

These ideas were incorporated into normative Rabbinic Judaism as well as Christianity and Islam. The Rabbis pick up this Neo-Platonism and

Aristotelian thinking through the exposure to the Greek source texts and later it is famously embraced by both Moses ben Nachman aka Nachmanides (1124 – 1270) and Moses ben Maimon aka Maimonides (1135-1204) who inspire the Kabbalists to import these philosophic ideas into the notion of Ayn Sof.

Hence Ayn Sof became considered as changeless, above and beyond the physical universe, immovable, and unaffected by any and all human and material things.

That idea of non-changing is of course in direct contradiction to Luria's creation myth and his concept of Tikkun Olam, but that paradox didn't bother him or the Rabbis who incorporated those ideas. They still held onto the idea of Ayn Sof as described by Neo-Platonists and Aristotle.

Additionally, science rejects the idea of the unchanging nature of the universe. Overall the Western ontology and metaphysics are directly contradictory to observable science.

Daoism embraces a notion of the Dao as feminine, changing, dynamic, living as a part of time, it is non-dual, it is soul and form, matter and spirit, matter and energy are co-equal and a part of the Infinite Dao, which gets expressed in Yin and Yang, and then emanates onward into the myriad beings of the physical universe.

I consider Ayn Sof as an equivalent of the Dao as described in the *Dao De Ching* of Lao Tzu.

This is why my idea of the Cosmos is not panentheistic (an oppositional duality of Mind/Spirit vs Body) but rather pantheistic (Mind/Spirit and the Body as a unity).

My idea of Ayn Sof explicitly acknowledges ideas that are implicit within the Lurianic myth that the creator is not all-knowing but limited, and is subject to change and imperfection, hence the creation of the finite structure of the Sefiroth and its disharmony is due to its act of creation, and lastly why Ayn Sof needs, and created humanity to take on Tikkun Olam since only humanity can change the Cosmos and the nature and essence of Ayn Sof as well.

The Tree is rooted and lives in the Rabbi's Gan Eden

The living environment, the mythic theology that I wish to offer recognizes that the Sefiroth was the tree that was created and placed in Gan Eden. The Sefiroth is the rabbinic 'world tree' of Gan Eden, aka the Garden of Eden. Hence the Sefiroth is the Cosmic Tree of Life and Knowledge that still stands at the center of creation in Gan Eden. It is there that we can connect to the Cosmos and the Divine by interacting with the Tree rooted in Gan Eden once we get beyond the Cherubim with his flaming sword that bars the entrance.

The Tree was created as a byproduct of the rabbinic vision of creation and the Garden of Eden tale. My intention is not to directly study Rabbinic Kabbalah as an ongoing spiritual practice, but rather to become familiar with it as a means to do the Occult work. I believe that once you have an understanding and appreciation of that mythic Rabbinic environment, then the work can become properly rooted and thus be more fulfilling. I also want to go beyond certain limitations within Rabbinic Judaism. I feel that the Rabbi's acceptance of Cosmic Evil, their occasional acceptance of oppositional duality concepts and influences, all need to be recognized and removed.

Let me begin by turning to the texts. The TaNaK, the Hebrew bible, is a literary product that started long ago before it became fixed in its final form. The TaNaK contains myth; by this, I mean that it is the sacred history of the Hebrews and the Judeans. It is not actual history, such as a history of the events of the American Revolution or the American Civil War, but it is told in the literary form of historical recounting. I believe that the start of the Rabbis, the TaNaK, and the Rabbinic project are to be found in the Babylonian Exile circa 597 BCE. The culmination and blossoming of the Rabbinic movement were during the time of the destruction of the Temple and the establishment of Yavneh academy around 70 CE.

Literally, we can start with the opening word of the TaNaK, Bereshith. This word can be translated as 'At the beginning' 'With the beginning', 'In the beginning', or 'By the beginning'. The Kabbalah Rabbis treat this opening word to allude to a host of events and processes that culminate with the creation of the universe as we now know it and inhabit it.

What did happen before our creation?

To hint at the answer there is a midrash associated with verse 36:31 in the first book of the Torah, '*And these are the kings that reigned in the land of*

Edom, before there reigned any king over the children of Israel.[22]' These eight kings

who existed before the children of Israel took on a mystical meaning beyond

the literal one. The literal meaning would read this to mean that before the

people of Israel had anointed Saul, there were the people in the land of

Edom who had a series of eight kings.

The mystical reading is that 'before ...the children of Israel' means

that there was a 'time' and a 'place' where there was no Israel, which they

took to mean a set of literal worlds (universes) prior to our world(universe)

that does have Israel in it, hence eight worlds (universes) were created in a

series of unsatisfactory creations. The rabbis imagined that eight times the

universe was made and destroyed before our universe came to be. That idea

is noted in the Midrashim text *Bereshith Rabba* sections 3:7and 9:1. That

becomes the root of a series of Kabbalistic speculations in the Zohar texts

and culminates in the mythic theology devised by Rabbi Isaac Luria, aka

ARI.

Within the mythology of ARI, even when our ninth and final

universe was in the process of being created in the form of the Sefiroth

spheres, at some point the forces could not be contained, and one of the

---

[22] (Jewish Publication Society 1917)

sefirahs shattered. In one version of the tale, this shattered sefirah was Din. Pieces of this shattered sphere were scattered across the cosmos and became the source of cosmic Evil due to the fact that these parts of the Divine were separated from their connection of the dynamic living source of the divine energy. They hardened into the klippot, shells, or shards of power that gave rise to evil.[23]

Now, it is true that the concept of cosmic Evil, that evil had a source that was supernatural and outside of humanity, was a belief common to the Hebrews, the Judeans, and the Rabbis. It is an important focus of the Zohar and in the teachings of ARI. However, I will be deliberately abandoning this age-old theme and concept. I do not believe in such a concept. I believe that evil is only a human creation, an aspect of human actions alone. Thus, I will remove this idea from my workings in the Occult Qabalah.

To emphasize this I shall have the Sefirah that is shattered not be Din but instead be Daat, Knowledge. The shards of Daat do not result in evil, but the shattering does create disharmony in the Sefiroth. The idea of cosmic disharmony is where my interpretation of the tale agrees with ARI.

---

[23] For further Rabbinic ideas of Cosmic Evil see Appendix, pp 234-238.

I will depart from his theology by not continuing with the idea of cosmic evil.

My idea of the shattered sphere being Daat stems from the GRA's tree and from the *Sefer Yetzirah* 1:4

> *Ten Sefiroth of Nothingness*
> *Ten and not nine*
> *Ten and not eleven*
> *Understanding with wisdom*
> *Be wise with Understanding*
> *Examine with them*
> *And probe from them*
> *Make (each) thing stand on its essence*
> *And make the Creator sit on His base.*[24]

One way to take this is to believe that there was pre-creation and pre-the-shattering of the spheres, going to be eleven sefirahs, Daat, being number eleven. Or another way to take this is that before creation Daat would have been part of the ten active aspects of the Divine but Malkuth was not part of the ten. Malkuth would not be counted since it was not an active part of the Divine. With the creation and the shattering of the spheres Daat having been shattered allowed for Malkuth to be an active part of the ten. I also take this to mean that Malkuth is not separated from the rest of the Tree. In the cosmos of the shattered spheres Malkuth, the place of the

---

[24] (Kaplan 1990, 38)

physical universe, is as much a part of the Divine as all the rest. Hence for me, the Cosmos and the Divine are one, this is a pantheistic cosmology. To assert a pantheistic concept of divinity is to side with Baruch Spinoza, who famously first proposed such an idea. This assertion of pantheism was I believe the reason why Spinoza was excommunicated by the Dutch Rabbinic community.

Rabbinic Judaism and the Kabbalistic Rabbis as well believed in a panentheistic cosmology. The map of the Territory called Panentheism is the idea that although the physical universe is created out of and is made up of, and is the body of the Divine, the Divine retains a fundamental separate nature from that body. The Divine is in its nature fundamentally above and beyond the physical. Panentheism is the cosmic equivalent of the mind-body split that Rene Descartes noticed and discussed. Under panentheism, the mind/God and the body/universe are two fundamentally different things and thus are not and cannot be equivalents.

I don't find that map to be useful nor do I find it to be an accurate description of the facts that describe the functioning of the mind and the body. Hence, I do not believe in the mind-body separation and split. I believe that the mind is a property that arises naturally out of the workings of the body. They are two aspects of the same thing. A person has a mind and a body. Alternatively, a person has mental attributes that can be noticed and described as the natural workings of the body[25].

Therefore, I do not maintain a cosmic mind-body split, which is what you create with the idea of panentheism. Instead, I believe in a pantheistic cosmos. Pantheism is the idea that the physical universe and the Divine are one and the same, a mind-body unity on a cosmic scale. I also believe in a finite and limited Divine[26], an entity that can and does make mistakes and cannot control every outcome and event.

I believe that the Divine, Ayn Sof, is not a separate entity, but the Divine and the cosmos are one and the same. Ayn Sof manifests as the Tao, the cosmic Way of the universe. Ayn Sof is the mind of the cosmos, with the physical universe is the cosmic body. The form of the Divine that we can understand and the form of the divine that resides within all things is called Shekinah.

---

[25] For an understanding of the facts as I accept them check out George Lakoff and Mark Johnson's *Philosophy in the Flesh: The Embodied Mind and its Challenge to Western Thought*, 1999.and Antonio Damasio's *Self Comes to Mind: Constructing the Conscious Brain*, 2010.

[26] William James in 1908 explored and presented such a concept of the divine, limited and pantheistic, in his series of lectures delivered at Manchester College, England. These he collected and published as *A Pluralistic Universe*, in 1909.

The Tree that would have been had creation not gone astray, was according to my myth, in the form of the GRA's tree that has Daat as one of the Sefirahs. However, the shattering of Daat left the cosmos with Ten Sefirahs and Daat no longer a part of the Tree. Hence, our tree is the ARI tree where the X marks the spot where once Daat resided.

The Sefiroth is not only the Tree of Life and Knowledge; it is the form of the Divine itself. Ayn Sof manifests itself into the cosmos in the form of this cosmic Tree.

The universe is created by the Divine through an act of failure, error, and in a sense, hubris. Resulting in the cosmic disharmony and the trapping of the Divine into a fixed form of disharmony and unbalance. This disharmony and unbalance requires some action to be taken that is done by a being that is part of creation. We, humanity, were created to repair the cosmos and the Divine, this action is called Tikkun Olam, Hebrew for Repair, Restoring, and the Fixing the World.

The GRA's Tree as the Hypothetical Plan of Ayn Sof

I offer the following insight.

Let's try to imagine what the cosmos would have looked like if, according to my tale of creation, Ayn Sof had been able to create the world without the breaking of the spheres.

My idea is that it would resemble the Tree as conceived and illustrated in the GRA's 1884 commentary on the *Sefer Yetzirah*. It would look like the figures on pages 115, 116, 156, and 175 of this book. Where the upper 10 Sefirahs would all be active and this configuration would be the blueprint, the DNA structure, of all created things that exist within Malkuth.

Yesod would be the womb and the vaginal birth opening for the creation of the physical universe that would be Malkuth. Everything would be in harmony. Malkuth would be the recipient of all the harmonious workings of the divine forces.

However, this was not to be. Ayn Sof was unable to create perfection and the sefirah Daat did shatter. The result was the disharmonious pattern of the cosmos that is represented by the Zohar/ARI tree, figures on page of this book 163, where Daat is just barely present on the tree structure and Malkuth is fully a part of the workings of the cosmos.

This Tree has the forces within Malkuth which can affect the total workings of the Divine and the cosmos. The beings, us humans, dwelling in Malkuth can effect change and transformation of all of the forces of the cosmos and the Sefiroth.

What follows is my retelling of ARI's creation myth explaining all of this.

Bereshith: My Mythic tale of Creation

This is not your Bubbe's story.

This is not your rabbi's story.

I'm doing the telling.

Bereshith.

In the beginning.

At the time of beginning.

As that story went…

Long ago before the first tick or tock…

Long ago before that big bang…

There simply was.

Flux.

Matter and energy were flitting back and forth, one into the other…playing like the Cheshire cats smile…coming and going.

For how long?

Who can say? Since no human mind was there to ask and answer the question.

Besides, there was no when in which to have the question formed, heard, or responded to.

There simply was.

However, as such story's go...there was somehow a moment when that was not enough.

Out of the continual something-ness, there came desire.

A want.

A hope.

We, in the here and now, hear and see the echoes of all of this. We can talk about it, even if it could not.

We can call this want Ayn Sof.

A Hebrew term that means no end, no limits, without end, without limits.

We can call it infinite.

We can call it infinity.

We can call it everything.

As Lao Tzu wrote to remind us that the name that can be given is not what it is. The name is not its totality. Names only point to being; they are not being in themselves.

As Alfred Korzybski reminds us, words are not the thing.

Nonetheless, we like names, and as deceptive as they can be, we need them to point towards something we want to talk about. And so, I will tell you about the story of Ayn Sof and Bereshith, at the time of beginnings.

So, as our story goes, all is Ayn Sof. It wove itself into existence out of its desire to be.

But, for it, it was not enough.

Desire consumed it and desire drove it.

Ayn Sof contracts inward.

Ayn Sof withdraws inward.

Leaving a place.

A void.

Desire encircles itself and it grows.

Desire was the seed and around it grew…

Simple though it was, stability and structure were formed.

And of course, then there was light.

Light fills the void and so we have what we can call a big bang.

It was the first bang, so it can pridefully proclaim itself 'big'.

The first sexual act.

The first climax.

The first orgasm.

Eventually, we will be able to listen to the sounds of that sex act to this day, like voyeurs, trying to imagine what it was like.

Except, we cannot hear the first orgasm, but we hear the orgasmic act out of which we came from.

It will make sense a bit later....

Anyway, after that heady first act, things were still simple.

Ayn Sof was more there than before.

But, this was not enough.

Once was not enough.

Desire built for more.

Desire to be more.

Desire to be others.

Desire to be with others.

And so He dreamed.

He dreamed of great things and He tried it out.

Something was made; we might call it a universe if it had a chance to be.

But, it wasn't good enough.

Poof. It was gone.

He tried again.

Another universe. Another garment to inhabit and to fill with beings.

No, that wasn't satisfactory either.

Poof, it was swallowed up and returned to the source, Ayn Sof.

Again.

Again.

Eight times in all.... (But then again who was counting?) everything was made and found wanting.

Enchanted with the act and indulged in it to create and be more, to be enough; to satisfy the desire.

Finally, in the act of forming a universe, He had enough structure and form to realize the potential of being and that filled Him with even greater desire.

A big complex dream formed.

A complex fixed static, yet dynamic, a finite garment of infinite being and infinite potential.

Wow. The lure of impossible and improvable and the desire to be was a rush.

A shape and pattern of 11 interlocking and interconnecting points of power, spheres of power, vessels, containers, they would be themselves, cloaks and garments for it to wear and to give it shape and form. He would engrave it into and out of a pattern of foundational numbers that are letters, in sets of 3 would be called mothers, and 7 would be doubles, with 12

remaining; all interlacing, interconnecting, channels to allow for an ever-

flowing, dynamic interactions. He gave it shape, form, and intentions. It

would be magnificent.

The vessels would eventually be called by names…of course since

He knew himself to be all-knowing, He knew is, was, and shall be, hence,

the echoes of the names bubbled up into awareness and He found the names

good. The first would be called Keter (Crown), the next, a pair would be

Hochmah (Wisdom), and Binah (Understanding), then Daat (Knowledge),

then the pair of Gedulah v' Chesed (Greatness of Lovingkindness) and

Gevurah V' Din (Power of Judgment), then Tifereth v' Rachamim (Beauty of

Compassion), then the pair of Netzach (Victory through Endurance) and

Hod (Majesty through Splendor), then Yesod (Foundation of procreative

center), and last but not the least it would all end in the burgeoning and

every growing Malkuth (The physical Queendom).

Swallowing this universe up and one last time, to get it right this

time, to explode into greatness, grandeur, and glory!

Our wondrous, big enormous orgasmic bang had finally occurred!

Riding the ways of orgasm, He sang out his form and it flowed.

Infinite being flowed into finite containers and rushed onward to form more channels and more containers, a rush of power and potency. The first vessel was formed and then the energy flowed and coalesced into the second vessel and then out the energy rushed out, headlong and the third vessel had to be quickly formed to contain it. Power surge and overflowed. Demanding to be let loose and with a bursting gush, it poured into what needed to be the fourth vessel.

Yet, it was all happening too fast, too quickly, the channels and containers were being built in haste, confidence and calm plans were being swept up in the headlong surge of relentless overwhelming force. That fourth vessel was just barely formed and already it was filled to the brim.

How did the next channels go? There was this plan....

The power surged and built up and it...

Could not contain it all.

Impossible had caught up to unlikely.

Improbable had climaxed to overwhelming flow and it could not be contained.

Gushing, rushing, overflowing, bursting, and billowing forth could not be contained long enough and so...another sort of bang.

The container that would be called Daat, exploded, shattered outward and all was about to be lost to chaos.

No! Cried out Ayn Sof, no, I cannot be stopped, I am in control. I am in control. I will have my way!

I know what I am doing!

I am in control.

I must be in control.

I will control….

Hastily there was a gathering of being and quickly forged was the remainder, a hint, a whiff, an essence of Daat was all that remained.

Forming and flowing and rushing and gushing, channels and vessels and containers made and filled and flowing and on and on it went.

All the infinite poured down into the last vessel and filled it and here it was allowed to expand. Here would be a place for a thing called life. A nest. A home.

Now, Ayn Sof was done. A home and a container for it had been built.

Ayn Sof rested and looked out at itself.

Where there was to be 11, He found only 10. The fourth vessel was fragmented and lost, shattered and scattered, only a hint of it remained.

Yet, it was done.

Yet the plan was achieved.

It must be good, right?

It was not right.

It didn't feel right.

The lost shattered sphere of being was hardening all around the spaces between.

The energy flowed but it was not balanced.

There was no peace.

There was only disharmony.

Ayn Sof was able to articulate and contemplate since matter and energy had pattern and structure. I will try again. I can get it right. I can do anything I want.

But....

NOOOO!

Impossible!

It cannot be!

For once Ayn Sof was stymied.

His desires were unmet and unfulfilled.

There was no pulling back.

There was no restarting.

No!

Trapped.

Fixed.

Contained.

No way to rearrange.

No pulling back.

Done.

It was fixed and complete.

Helplessness.

Stuck.

Trapped.

Anguish.

Despair.

In its bottom vessel, life was where a universe was now starting.

Ticks had been following tocks.

Space and time were and would always be.

That was okay. But, it was not quite right. It hadn't gone as planned.

I am stuck. I need to fix this.

Ayn Sof tries with all its being, with all its power, with all its desire, will all its needs, will all its will…and….nothing happens.

I cannot.

Despair. Doom. Desolation.

But, wait.

Yet, it felt the beating heart of some things, many things, and living

things.

I have made a place for life.

Where there is life, I feel there dwells hope.

Perhaps there can be a way. I can still create. I need beings

I will make others who can.

They will make it right for my sake and for theirs.

They must.

The song of Tikkun Olam was heard throughout the universe and

it was calling out to be heard.

The song of repair.

The song of restoration.

The song of hope.

Can you hear it?

Some theological implications from this Creation Myth

I believe this story has many implications and most of them are not overtly recognized by the Rabbis who have accepted ARI's story.

Let us start with the nature of the Divine. The Biblical and Rabbinic God is considered all-powerful and all-knowing. Those attributes are difficult for me to accept when I consider the story.

By way of analogy, when I engage in a creative act I often create a draft and after considering it later, I discard it as unsatisfactory when I realize it did not meet my intentions or did not meet them completely. This process of creating draft versions, discarding them, and revising them is a common occurrence and a natural one. However it makes sense, I am a simple finite creature with many limitations. I need to try things out for me to see the outcome and consider what I made.

It doesn't make sense that a supposedly infinite being with infinite unlimited knowledge and wisdom could fail not once but nine times in total. With the ninth creative act being a fatal one, this so-called infinite all-knowing and all-wise being is trapped by the failure of the act of creation. If God was supposedly all-knowing, could It not have seen the problems before It acted and thus avoided the mistake? How can an all-knowing God find itself trapped in a situation of its own making? Unless of course it deliberately trapped itself to create the problem that makes creating humanity a necessary solution? That is a possibility, but I prefer a fallible deity.

I prefer the idea that Ayn Sof as described in the creation tale of ARI that I am adopting is not all-knowing and all-wise. Ayn Sof is in actuality a being of limits, a being that can and does make mistakes. A being of infinite parameters and dimension but not of infinite power. A deity that is fallible, that cannot foresee an outcome and thus can be caught and trapped. A deity that needs help, assistance, and rescuing.

Now you may have noticed in my telling, that I referred to Ayn Sof, sometimes as 'It', sometimes as 'He' and sometimes as 'She'. That is due to my own playful recognition of my own bias. The use of *It* stems from considering the Divine as beyond human form and typology. *She* stems from applying some of the characteristics of the Dao to Ayn Sof; also the use of the feminine is to invoke the wise mother persona. Lastly, my use of the masculine is that I imagine 'only' a guy could be this kind of a schlemiel, one of those guys in his garage coming up with this way-too-complicated-thing and believing he is capable of building anything and "why bother reading the instructions that it comes with" and then having it all blow up in his face. Lastly, I will continue the mixing of the male and female pronouns to refer to the deity in the Gan Eden story. When the deity is being overly complicated and controlling I will refer to it by the male pronoun. When the deity is being wise and looking at the big organic whole picture I will refer to it by the feminine pronoun. That's my own bias at play.

Lastly, Daat was the sefirah that shattered. But shards and remnants remain. They are scattered throughout the cosmos in the realms surrounding the Sefiroth. Also the fruit of 'The Tree' in the garden from which Eve and Adam ultimately eat. That fruit is bits of Daat.

The Myth of Gan Eden

So again, this is not your Bubbah's story.

Nor, is it your Rabbi's story.

I'm doing the telling...

Well...after the mess that Ayn Sof made of the cosmos there was a need for some damage control. The dream and hope of Tikkun Olam were sung out into the cosmos.

Within Malkuth, there was a collection of stars being formed and they eventually joined to form a galaxy. Within a spiral of that galaxy was an ordinary unpretentious little yellow star and its planets were forming. Here, life was taking hold.

Eventually, there would be hominids, that's what they would be called, who could walk the face of the third planet from that star.

For this little star, Ayn Sof started to weave a particular form for Herself, a means to dwell within this place. She was doing this all across the cosmos wherever she found the possibility of life. Each little cosmic nest got its own specific indwelling aspect of the infinite being that is Ayn Sof.

Our story concerns that specific yellow star in a specific spiral galaxy. This form of Ayn Sof that dwelt in this place some would call her

Shekinah.

Shekinah realized that these hominids could become the tools for what She needed at this spot in the cosmos. These hominids could hear the song and take up its tune. They could help in repairing, restoring, and healing the cosmos and by doing so, heal, restore, and repair Ayn Sof, Herself. If only they would listen and agree to help.

Shekinah began to think.

To plot, plan, and scheme.

From all these scheming thoughts, He created an elaborate story song just for them.

He would sing a song of their beginning, a sweet little *just-so* story to tell around the fires and to pass down. This scheme would convince them to answer the call of Tikkun Olam. It would be perfect. He was certain of it.

He knew that they would call it 'The Gan Eden story' when they evolved to have a language to tell such things to themselves.

So, He started to tinker with a group of them who were struggling to make a life for themselves on the savannah. He helped them to go from simple hominid to Homo sapiens.

He made up a story to tell them. It would be great. It would impress them and inspire them. He thought, a little embellishment here and there, is always a good idea. He needed them to accept their condition, that everything would grow old and one day dies, and that they needed to have responsibility for themselves, each other, and the Cosmos itself. That they were specially created to do what no other being could do. That they were not just physical beings but had within them a spark of the Cosmos, of the Divine, that meant that they mattered, they were needed, and they were a part of the answer. They needed to hear and willingly respond to the song of Tikkun.

And so, here is that story…

"Once upon a time, there was a God who decided He wanted helpmates. And so He schemed. He created a womb, a birthplace, it would be in the form of a comfortable and bountiful garden. A perfect place where everything would be happy and content. A cozy little temporary dwelling contained within warm water. An island paradise with a garden in its center. There in the center will be found the root of the cosmic tree. A grand, glorious, gleaming, dazzling, radiant tree. It was the likeness and image of the splendor that is the Divine. It was the Tree of Life and Knowledge for all to see, to admire and to be awestruck by its brilliance. It will be like a model of his grand self, 9 spheres of light and power with 21 interlocking and interconnecting pathways. One last path leads downward from the ninth sphere to lodge in the bottommost glowing globe that was half-buried in the

soil. And hanging from the tree, at the center of the upper section of the tree

was a single piece of fruit. That fruit was a delight to the eyes and it was

special. It was both a treat and a bit of a trick.

And so God said 'Let there be light!' and the show began."

(He was particularly pleased with that bit. The story continues…)

"God said 'Let there be a heaven! Let there be an Earth for life to

dwell upon! Let there be grass, herbs and fruit trees! And they were good.

I'll make all sorts of animals, male and female for all of them. Let there be

swimming creatures and flying creatures! And they were good. Let there be

animals who walk and crawl on land! And they were good.

And then God said, 'Let us make creatures in our image, after our

likeness."

(He was particularly pleased with inventing what would be called,

the Royal 'we'. After all, He was the grand and glorious creator and ruler

over all. He should sound lofty and important. He thought the use of the

plural will impress them. The story continues…)

"Let them have dominion over all living things, they can be like us,

like little rulers."

And so God went to the center of the land and in the shadow of the cosmic tree, he crafted out of the stuff of the Earth two humans, a male, and female. Two creatures to walk upright. Different but equal they will be. He gave them names, the male was pale-skinned like the sandy beach and light of hair, while the female her skin was the color of the rich soil and hair as dark as night. God had crafted well. They were beautiful. He bent down, kissed them, and breathed into them to fill them with his breath of life, and they awoke to life. He took their hands and helped them to stand up. "You," God said gesturing to the male, "will be called Adam, and you," God said gesturing to the female, "will be called Lilith."

And God said "Gather around everyone and everything! Come here and be here now!"

And all the things that traveled on the land, all the things that flew and all the things that could swim, all gathered close to listen. Once everyone was settled down, God smiled and began to speak to them all. "Hear me now, all things that fly, swim, creep, and walk, listen to me well. I am God, your creator. Behold, there are fresh springs and rivers of cool refreshing water to drink. I have given you every herb yielding seed, which is upon the face of all the earth, and every tree, in which is the fruit of a tree yielding seed—to you, it shall be for food; and to every beast of the earth, and to every fowl of the air, and to everything that creeps upon the earth, and also to my special children, Adam and Lilith." God pointed at the two of them, "So, to all, I say to you all; behold this day is very good! Go and eat, drink and be merry, for tomorrow you will...." And God smiled ever so sweetly with a gleam and a wink and continued. "Well...tomorrow, I'm sure it will be just another ordinary day. Oh, and one more thing, here is something to ponder, it's a riddle from one of your ancestors to be, his name is Rabbi Hillel. He said this: If you are not for yourself, who will be. If you are for yourself alone, what are you? And if not now, when. "

Adam and Lilith looked at God a bit confused but then God vanished and they were alone with all the pairs of the other animals who were enjoying being there in the warmth and were cuddled up together.

"What is this 'ancestor' thing he was talking about?" Adam asked. "For that matter, there was a lot of what he was saying that didn't make sense."

Lilith looked at Adam and smiled. "I'm sure it will all make sense eventually."

So Lilith came to lie next to Adam, and their warm soft bare flesh touched and they noticed that this was good. As they touched, Adam was aroused and Lilith had a happy thought, smiled and she straddled Adam to mount him and they shared each other.

Afterward, while Adam slept, Lilith got up and went off to examine the glowing cosmic Tree that was in the center of everything.

She walked around it and studied it intently. She felts its radiance and its power. She touched it and she was changed. She felt herself joining with it like she had joined with Adam earlier. She felt joy and questions were answered. She learned about how life is, was, and shall be, at least how it was planned out for her and Adam. She learned about how and when they left this garden that then the joining of flesh would eventually lead to new life being created out of her flesh. How this act of creation mimicked the act of creation that brought all things into being. She learned about the shattering and she heard Shekinah's song.

All in all, it flowed into her and in a blink of her eye. Then the connection ended and she could feel and hear the beating of her heart.

"Hmm," she thought and considered. "Well, I can choose my own destiny. I have knowledge and power. Adam's nice, but I'm no one's vessel for creation."

And with that thought, she gathered in her newfound knowledge and power, and in a burst of light, she left.

And God saw this and said: "It is not good that the man should be alone; this will not do. I will make him a help meet for him."

Adam awoke and asked God, "Where is Lilith?"

"Lilith has left," God says. "Let us play a game together. It is called the naming game. I will show you things and you will give them a name."

God pointed out all the plants and trees and told Adam a few things them and from this Adam was prompted to give it a name.

God said, "Of every tree of the garden you may freely eat; but of the tree of the knowledge and life, you should not eat of it; for in the day that you eat of it you will realize that you have within you the seed of death."

"What is a day? What is a seed? And what is…," Adam asked.

"Later, it will make sense. Let us continue the naming game," God said.

Adam forgot his questions since he was too excited in the act of giving things names. As every beast of the field and every fowl of the air; came over, for Adam to see and be told a few things about them, and whatsoever the man would call every living creature that was to be the name thereof. And he gave names to all cattle, and to the fowl of the air, and to every beast of the field.

"I have noticed that all creatures that you made were mated pairs of male and female, but now that Lilith you say has left," Adam said, and thought to himself, whatever that means, "I have no other to pair with."

"This is true. Lie down and close your eyes and I will take care of this," God said.

While Adam slept God took from him a bone, and out of that he forged a new being, one God thought will stick with Adam, as once did this bit of his flesh.

Adam awoke and saw a woman with the rich tones of inner flesh and hair the color of dark blood lying next to him. And she awoke and smiled brightly at the sight of Adam.

"Adam meet Eve. She will be your companion. Now, I will leave you two to get to know each other. Eve, my dear, listen to Adam and he will explain all that you need to know. At least for now."

With that God departed.

"Tell me everything!" Eve said.

And so Adam did, as much as he could remember. He told her about Rabbi Hillel, though he didn't know what 'Rabbi' meant, and he was very proud that he could remember Hillel's saying, he told her about how he got to name things, and he showed her all the plants and creatures and told them their names. He told her that all the plants and fruit on the trees were good to eat. He told her about 'death' that scary-sounding unknown, and how surly they would catch death on the day they touched the Trees of

Knowledge or Life. And lastly, when they came back to lie under the Cosmic Tree, he explained how to cuddle and become one and truly know someone.

After they rested from their knowing each other repeatedly, Eve got up and looked upon the Cosmic Tree. Through the radiance, she saw that it was composed of 10 spheres altogether connected by branches and a trunk that was 22 in number. But she did not touch it, not being sure of that unknown thing death.

Adam joined her and said, "Aren't they magnificent? They surely must be the Tree of Knowledge and the Tree of Life that God had told us about."

"Trees?" Eve said.

"Can't you see them? I know the light is a bit blinding and it is hard to make out, but there are two trees that are in the center of everything," Adam explained.

Eve thought to herself, I see only one tree. He seems to see two, why? "Tell me what you see."

And Adam does. He points out that they are similar but different. He points out that somehow he knows the names of the spheres, he points out that the Tree of Knowledge has the sphere of Daat, knowledge, at the bottom of the upper set of four, while the Tree of Life has a shining cluster of fruit hanging at the center of intersecting branches where Daat would

have been. How the configuration of the branches in each are 3 horizontal,

7 vertical, counting the trunk as one of the vertical, and that there are 12

diagonal branches; though the overall arrangements are different.

Eve listens with puzzled wonder that he sees something much

different than she. He has divided the single tree into two, as far as she can

tell. She can see in the dynamic fluctuations of energy that the configuration

he describes is created as the Tree phases with the energy flow.

Eve asks, "Adam, the light is so bright and it seems to flicker so, do

you see that too?"

"No. It is just an almost overwhelming steady glow. All are solid,

strong, and continuous. Why?"

"Oh, you're right. It just is hard to see through the light."

"It just takes time, I guess to see it right. Shall we go? I'm getting

hungry."

They wander off and Eve considers what it means that Adam sees

things differently from her.

They spend time, eating, playing with other animals, once again

getting to know each other, and resting from their exhausting knowing, then

going off to find something new to eat.

God looks upon this and is impatient. He was sure that by saying 'don't do this' that they would go off and do that. He thought he gave them curiosity, amongst his many gifts of inclinations. Time is passing, it seems that this day could end and they would have to leave this womb of a garden and be born into the real world without them eating the fruit of The Tree of Life and Knowledge. I need to prod things along.

So God made a new being. Dark and sleek like Lilith his skin was, though he was very, very male. God endowed the Serpent more than he had Adam. The Serpent was a creature whose skin was warm to the touch, though he was cold-blooded. His name was Serpent. He was a magnificent male animal. God was certain that he would do the trick. God explained how things were and about the notion that eating from the fruit of the Tree of Knowledge and Life would bestow knowledge and wisdom, and they would then realize that all things must die.

God introduced Serpent to Adam and Eve. And Adam and the Serpent both saw that they were alike, they were two males of the same kind, and there was only one female.

Eve looked upon Serpent and wondered what it would be like to know him as she did Adam, it would be the same but just a bit more, and she smiled as she wondered what that would be like.

Adam saw that Serpent was overall bigger than he, and the Serpent smiled to show that he knew that as well. Adam held Eve closer to him as they stood there. Within them, both grew feelings of envy and jealousy.

This is good, God thought as he left them.

Eve took the Serpent's hand and said: "Let us go for a walk and see and explore and we can each take time to get to know each other better." The Serpent agreed and so did Adam.

And they did, each taking time to get to know the other, while they did, the Serpent realized that he was attracted to Adam, as much Eve, and so they all came to know each other.

While they all rested, the Serpent thought and schemed.

While Adam rested, Serpent took Eve off alone, and they went for a walk. He said to Eve, "Did God say it was alright to eat all the fruit from any tree in this garden?"

Eve replied, "Of the fruit of the trees of the garden we may eat; but of the fruit of the tree which is in the middle of the garden that special tree, I was told that God had said, 'You shall not eat of it, neither shall you touch it, lest you die."

The serpent said, "What is death, but something we know nothing about. What I think is that if we eat of the fruit, we will gain its property, it will open our eyes, we shall be as God, knowing all. Does that make sense? Is it not the fruit of the Tree of Knowledge?"

Eve looked at the tree and thought about that.

The Serpent left Eve to think and he returned to be with Adam once again.

Eve saw that the tree was good for food and that it was a delight to the eyes, and she concluded that the tree should be able to make one wise. She reasoned that this is what Lilith, the prior companion to Adam must have done. So, Eve climbed the tree. When she did she became one with the tree.

All things stopped or so it seemed to her, though the sun was starting to set.

She was filled with wonder. She understood. She understood how and why she was different than Adam and the Serpent, she understood the riddle of Hillel and that this place was a riddle as well. She had knowledge and wisdom. She knew now that their time here was coming to an end and what their destiny must be, to leave this place of birth and make their way in the wider world beyond. She heard clearly the song of Tikkun Olam and know of Shekinah, who was God but more so.

She agreed with it all and she knew that this would be good, at least as much as she could understand of what she felt.

She took a bite of the fruit and it was good.

She wanted to share what she had learned with Adam and Serpent.

The sky was glowing reddish and the air was cooling as she went and found Adam first. He was alone.

She offered Adam the fruit, and he took it and ate some of it. As she watched Adam eat, within Eve, the fear of death grew strong.

God saw this all and found it very good.

He called out to Adam and Eve, telling them to come to him.

They did so; Eve explained what that fruit was and where it came from. Fear grew now strong within them both. And so in fear they hid. The air was cool and they shivered. They made coverings for them to keep warm, and as they did this they realized that they had been naked and now they were not.

And God called to Adam, "Where are come you? Come to me."

Adam came out of hiding wearing his covering and stood before God.

"Why are you covered up like this?" God asked.

Adam said, "I was naked before and now I need to cover myself."

God said, "Who told you that you were naked?"

"I don't know. I just had this knowledge in me," Adam explained.

God asked "You have this knowledge, is that because you ate of the Tree?

Adam replied, "Eve, who you gave to me, gave to me the fruit of the tree and I did eat it."

God called out to Eve, "Show yourself and come here."

Fear was strong within her; she shivered more from the fear than from the cool air as she approached.

God asked, "What is this that you have done?"

Fear gripped her and she did not know what to think and she had heard what Adam had said and so she said, "The Serpent spoke to me about the tree and I did eat."

All this time Serpent had been nearby and heard and saw all that had occurred. He stood up and showed himself. He was still naked since the cool air did not bother him.

Before he could speak, God said to Serpent, "Because you have done what needed to be done, your task is complete. Now you will take on your true form, upon thy belly shall you go, and dust shalt you eat all the days of your life. And you will be remembered as a symbol of having to leave the garden. Seeing you will forever remind them of the awakening to the experience of death and hardship, and so they will feel an enmity between you and the woman, and between your offspring seed and hers, they shall bruise your head, and you shall bruise their heel."

They watched as Serpent glowed and transformed. He became smaller and slender and now no longer looked like them. Of his limbs they were all gone, one coiling body he now had. Then another like him was made, a female of his species was formed from the earth. The two, male and female serpents slithered off together.

Unto Eve God said, "You will discover that in pain you will you bring forth children; and your desire shall be to Adam, who will be your husband, and he shall be the one to tell you what to do."

Unto Adam God said, "'because you had not considered on your own and you only hearkened unto the voice of Eve, your wife, and you have hastily eaten of the tree, you shall feel that you are responsible and feel guilty. So you will feel that you are cursed. You will experience life as toil and hardship. Thorns also and thistles shall you discover, hardship will you feel. In the sweat of your face shall you eat bread, till you return unto the ground; for out of it you were taken. For dust you are and unto dust shall you return. As I had told you, this day has come to an end. That is why darkness is covering the face of the land."

Adam and Eve shivered and wept.

God said, "Behold, you have become as I, you have the seed of knowledge within you. However, hearing what you have told me, We realize that you are not yet ready to take again from the Tree of Life and Knowledge. There are many things you must experience and learn first. To do this you must be born into the world, and so you must leave here. "

Therefore, God sent them forth from the Garden of Eden, to till the ground from whence they were taken. He placed an idea within them to keep them from returning till they had first learned wisdom. And so at the east of the Garden of Eden, they imagined there was a being, a cherubim, who had a flaming sword, which turned every way, and so they assumed this was why they could not return.

As they departed from the Garden and found the lands beyond different but similar, they comforted each other as they went off in search of shelter. Eve told Adam what she learned from the Tree, told him, that she knew it was one tree, and told him about the song that Shekinah, the creator of all, had sung out for all to hear. She told him that it was a song of hope and of healing. And she sang it to him. They found comfort in it and they found it very good.

It was evening; the sixth day of creation had come to its end, and God said it was very good.[27]

---

[27] For an afterward of this story see Appendix 1 on page 223.

Some theological implications of this Gan Eden myth

What I'm about to say should not be interpreted as being a statement concerning the essence or fundamental nature of humans or of any specific gender. It is all said in the context of explaining that myth. I used them as archetypes to represent types of choices and I choose certain characters within the myth to embody that choice.

Now, we sometimes tell ourselves stories to explain what we don't like, to make excuses for what we have to face up to, to find a way to blame others, to justify, to say it's not my fault, I'm not responsible. That is the essence of the Scapegoat mentality. I wish to go beyond it.

The Garden of Eden story was often told in that manner and thought of in that way. A Deity of limitations through its own mistrust of its creation believed that it needed to trick and deceive because it was not certain that it would find willing helpers and it was desperate, that explains my myth.

Let's face it death is natural and inevitable, but we don't like it. The Garden tale gave us an excuse and out, if only things were different, we wouldn't have to die.

I see the Garden as a metaphor for the womb, a dwelling place where time does not yet exist for us. So long as we are in the womb we are not part of the world. It is only at birth do we come to face the inevitable reality of our death.

Many of us need the devil because we need someone other than ourselves to blame. However, it need not be this way.

If my version of the Lurianic myth of creation is accepted then we are needed and the Garden tale becomes of the story of how we came to be, how we were born to be. We are part of the finite and of the infinite. We are divine and ordinary. We have potential if only we act and are willing to accept our part in the cosmic story. If we are willing to help make things better.

In the context of the story, the Garden then is simply our cosmic womb from which we will and must inevitably leave. A place of intimate connection where everything is provided but we are not conscious we are utterly passive, waiting to become.

I have recast the tale, to remove excuses, so that we have the opportunity to acknowledge our destiny and to accept it and therefore to acknowledge our hope for potential, our ability to contribute once we awaken to our responsibilities to ourselves, to each other, to our planet and the cosmic Divine.

In the context of working with the myth, the Garden is the birthplace of all our thoughts, fears, hopes, and of course, dreams. It is the realm of our unconscious—singular and personal as well as our collective. It is the dream realm. In our context, it is not some place we lost but someplace we had to leave. It is the place of our birth, and hence where all things for us have a beginning, a start, a place of gestation before manifestation. The Garden is where we can always go back to but never stay in. It is where we can do the magick to connect with the cosmic Tree and thus stimulate Tikkun Olam.

Actually, every night we return to the Garden, our realm of the unconscious. With magick and imagination, we can go there as well.

In my story, God is young, limited in knowledge-i.e. not all-knowing. Can and does make mistakes. God, like us, just does as well as she can. God in my story is making it up as she goes along. She knows what she needs; she needs beings with the power and the knowledge to help with Tikkun, who freely chooses. She needs a community, hence the need for mothers and fathers to pass down the knowledge and teach. But she just tries things out and sees what happens, and meddles if the outcome is not going along with what she needs.

As for the story and its players, well here are some ideas.

In my story, I have turned the main characters into metaphors and symbols. Lilith, Adam, and Eve represent a continuum of choices. The continuum of self and the community. Where the negative extremes are the selfishness of a sociopath and the self-sacrifice of martyrdom. My characters are not that extremes, but they are the potential endpoints that could go over the edge and travel to the extremes. Therefore, I need someone to represent the 'inappropriate' choices, the choice that would not respond to the challenge and request to participate in Tikkun Olam. I pick on Lilith and Adam to be those examples.

Lilith is the one who chooses to be for herself alone. She could be a narcissist, at worst, or at least self-centered. Whereas Adam and Eve are two ways to support the community and not be for the self alone. However, Adam represents the follower of authority and so is not the way. He is also the one when he does lead, gets into the notion of hierarchy and control. Where one dominates over the other. Another not so good of a choice. Eve represents the one who believes that all should have a voice and cooperation is the key to communal success.

Metaphorically I used Adam and Eve to represent two world views. Adam is the view of the world that sees black and white, the oppositional duality of Aristotelian logic (i.e. no middle ground and non-contradiction), separateness, division, dissection, the assumption of complete knowledge, either-or as the only option. Whereas Eve is the holistic, non-dualism of Taoism, non-Aristotelian logic (contexts determine the outcome and the analysis, middle ground, and seeming contradiction that is resolved in shifting perspectives and recognition of multiple contexts), the acceptance of limited knowledge and incomplete knowledge, the combinational choice of 'and', the viewing of a living thing in its environment.

In my story Lilith and Adam are equals but Adam does not act, Lilith does. She figures things out but chooses to go her own way to seek for herself and so leaves the Garden without Adam.

Initially, Lilith metaphorically represents the Occult Qabalists in the old way of doing things. She is looking for knowledge and power to use but not to offer to others in support of some community goal, i.e. Tikkun Olam.

This leaves God to go back to the drawing board and make Eve.

Yet, they don't at first do anything but enjoy themselves. Again, the clock is ticking, they will at the end of the day be born and they need to learn about the Tree and its power to heal. So, God creates the Serpent, an animal who looks like a human and can interact sexually with Adam and Eve. God places him in the Garden to be a catalyst and hoping he will stir things up and get things to happen. God in my story lets him in on the plan, just a bit. He is told that he is put there to create change. To potentially create a push for Adam or Eve to seek out the Tree as a means to some end.

The serpent, in the end, is rewarded by God for his contribution but silenced before he can say what he knows. God didn't want Adam and Eve to know that they were being manipulated and that is what the serpent would have said, given the chance, and so he wasn't given the chance.

Now, what about the flaming sword? Why are we dealing with the flaming sword? Well, for one thing, it is part of the myth as recounted in TaNaK. So it is a symbol we should think about. At the end of the myth, it seems like Adam and Eve are being punished. Well, God is disappointed in them and their choices. Adam failed to think on his own, and thus did not set the best of examples. Eve, who heroically figured out the riddle of the garden and gets it all right, still at the end when asked why she ate of the Daat fruit, blew it. She doesn't give all those wonderful reasons that she had for doing what she did; she doesn't say she figured things out she panics. She lets fear, guilt, shame, and her lack of experience overwhelm her emotionally, and hence in a panic, she points to the Serpent. So, God is disappointed. And God sets the Cherubim with the flaming sword as a guardian at the gates of Gan Eden. It seems to bar the way. However, it only keeps out the foolish, the uninitiated. If you don't understand the mysteries, then you don't know the right words to say and the guardian will prevent you from entering. All you require is wisdom, the right understanding of what happened at Gan Eden and at failed to happen. Hence, you who are reading this book, who have studied and learned can become an initiate and thus return to the garden with wisdom, experience, courage, and pride.

In the end, as it is recorded in the first chapter, the events start with the sunset on the fifth day and end with the evening of the next day, which is the sixth day, that is the time when the events that take place in Gan Eden occur. They leave the Garden before the setting of the sun of that day. With the exiting from Gan Eden, they are born into the real world. It was recorded thusly about this day in Genesis 1:31 'And God saw everything that He had made, and behold, it was very good. And there was evening and there was morning, the sixth day.'

The Key to the Paths

Rather than rely on the fabrication of the Christian Jesuit Athanasius Kircher who had no respect for the material he was stealing and using, I wish to start by returning to the true source material of the Rabbis.

The historical key text turns out to be the shortest and most accessible of the Kabbalistic texts. It is the foundation upon which all the rest of the Kabbalah was built. It is the *Sefer Yetzirah, the Book of Formation*. In accordance with the *Sefer Yetzirah,* there is laid out that the key to unlocking the building blocks of creation is the letters of the Hebrew alphabet. The text presents a simple and clear understanding of the structure and pattern that the letters of the Hebrew alphabet are organized in. This pattern is the following:

There are 3 Primary letters called the Mother letters. They are Alef, Mem, and Shin. Roughly speaking these are the first, middle, and last letters of the alphabet.

Then there are 7 letters that have two ways to be articulated, these are the Double letters: Bet, Gimmel, Dalet, Kaf, Peh, Resh, and Tav. It is important to realize that in actuality only six of those letters truly have two ways to pronounce them, a hard and a soft-sounding method depending on the grammatical rules concerning the dagesh which designates these different sounds for the letters. The Resh is included amongst them due to a series of textual mistakes in the text of the Hebrew Bible[28]. I imagine that a scribe made an error and mistook the Resh for the letter Dalet and thus

---

[28] (Kaplan 1990, 160)

marked the Resh as if it were a double-sounding letter, thus getting a dagesh. This was done fourteen times with ten specific Hebrew words.[29] The rabbi who was the author of the *Sefer Yetzirah* had to have known this and treated the text as sacred and thus counted the Resh as one of the double letters.

There are the remaining 12 Letters, referred to as the 'Elemental' letters. (The term Elemental has no association to the four elements as understood by the Occult tradition.) These letters are Heh, Vav, Zayin, Chet, Tet, Yod, Lamed, Nun, Samekh, Eyin, Tzadi, and Kuf

In the Sefiroth diagram, there are 3 Horizontal paths, there are 7 Vertical paths and there are 12 Diagonal paths.

Recognizing this, the rabbinic kabbalists assigned the 3 Mother letters to the 3 Horizontal lines, the 7 Double letters to the 7 vertical lines, and the 12 Elemental letters to the 12 diagonal lines.

This is the first step in the logic used by the Kabbalists of how the Hebrew letters are assigned to the 22 paths. The next step is based on the shape of the array.[30]

---

[29] See Chart on page 160 of Kaplan's Sefer Yetzirah. First Samuel 1:6, 10:24, 17:25, Second Kings 6:32, Jeremiah 39:12, Proverbs 3:8, 11:21, 14:10, 15:1, 20:22, Ezekiel 16:4 in two words, Habakkuk 3:13, and Song of Songs 5:2.

[30] (Kupperman 2009) This article by Kupperman is another and different attempt to associate the Hebrew letters to the Tree. He also starts with the Aryeh Kaplan's *Sefer Yetzirah* but he does not acknowledge the GRA's tree that is illustrated in Kaplan's book. He states that 'for the exact placement, we will also turn to the earliest of the kabalistic texts, the Sefer Ha-Bahir.'(p.5) He uses Kaplan's translation of this text and his own intuition as well. He ends up with a different arrangement. It is complicated and requires reference to and intimate knowledge and study of Rabbinic

The array published in 1884 with the text of the Sefer Yetzirah written with commentary of the GRA, rabbi Eliahu ben Shlomo (April 23, 1720- October 9, 1797), the Gaon (Hebrew for genius) of Vilna, has his letters is presented as Figure 4 & 6 in this book and my drawing of it as Figure 5 & 9. This figure was presented on the cover of Aryeh Kaplan's *Sefer Yetzirah* as well as on page 31 of that book.

---

texts. In the end I find that it is too much effort and work to recall his explainations. Which is why I do not recommend it. I believe the GRA's system is the most natural, easiest to understand.

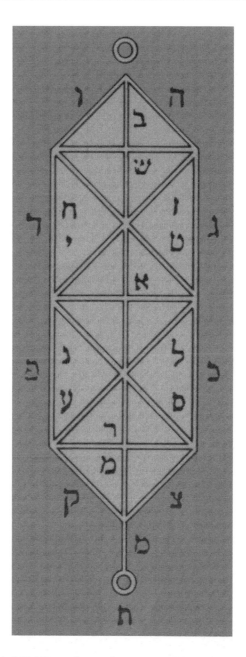

Figure 4: GRA 1884 Tree from the cover of Kaplan's Sefer Yetzirah

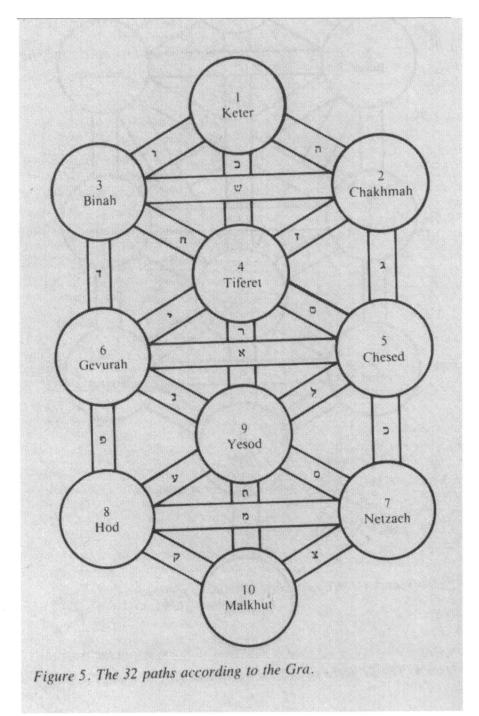

Figure 5. The 32 paths according to the Gra.

Figure 5: Kaplan's 'The 32 paths according to the GRA"

Now another and different array of the Tree is from the Zohar and is used in the *Pardes Rimmonim* (the *Orchard of Pomegranates*) of Rabbi Moses Cordovero. I believe that this Zohar-based array of the Sefiroth was derived from a two-step process. The first was it was based on *First Chronicles* 29:11 'Yours O God are the Greatness [Gedulah], the Strength [Gevurah], the Beauty [Tifereth], the Victory [Netzach], and the Splendor [Hod], for All in heaven and in earth; Yours O God is the Kingdom [Malkuth].'[31]

Noticed the sequence of how they are listed in the passage from *First Chronicles*, the sequence is listed as Greatness, Strength, and then Beauty. This means that Beauty is below the pair of Greatness and Strength. We now have the array as illustrated in Rabbi Joseph Gikatilla's *Sha'are Orah*.

As for placing the letters onto the Zohar array, I will do so based on the logic as presented by the 1884 array of the GRA and this is this system that I will use for our Qabalah project. I believe that it would be an acceptable solution to use a modification of GRA's logic and pattern. The GRA's logic is very accessible to the Western mind for it is a very top to bottom and left to right logic in his assignment of the letters. As for the Zohar array as created by ARI (Rabbi Isaac Luria) with his placement of the Hebrew letters on the Tree, I shall not use his system. Rather I will defer to The GRA's logic for the placement of the letters and this will take some explaining to make his decisions understandable.

Historically the Sephardic Gikatilla's *Sha' are Orah*'s array was first. This array was taken up by the Moses de Leon's *Zohar*, then by rabbi Cordovero's Pardes Rimonim, and finally by rabbi ARI.

---

[31] (Jewish Publication Society 1917)

How did they all assign the letters? What was the basis of their logic?

The first clue to that question is to go to the *Sefer Yetzirah* and realize the pattern of the three groupings of the Hebrew letters. Then to take this pattern and work with it to assign it to the paths of the Tree. Now, the 3 Mother letters clearly get assigned to the three horizontal lines of the Sefiroth.

In actuality, there seem to be two different systems, one drawn from the text and commentary of the *Bahir* and another system based on the text and commentary of the *Sefer Yetzirah*. It is clear that the three Mother letters are to be placed on the three horizontal paths of the Sefiroth. The question is which of the Mother letters go on which path?

One answer according to the *Bahir* is the following. According to the commentary the Alef is placed at the topmost horizontal path between Hochmah and Binah, Mem to the middle horizontal path between Chesed and Din, and Shin to the lowest horizontal path between Netzach and Hod. This logic is given credence in the commentary notes that Kaplan gives to the text of the *Bahir*.

'Alef is usually said to represent Keter-Crown. Actually, the "Holy Palace" is the confluence of the four basic concepts, Keter-Crown, Chokmah-Wisdom, Binah-Understanding, and Malkuth-Kingship, and it is seen as the center point of the six Sefiroth of Zer Anpin. The four concepts are denoted by the four corners of the Alef. Furthermore, in the diagram of the Thirty-Two Paths, Alef is the channel between Chakmah-Wisdom and Binah-Understanding.'[32]

'Shin represents the confluence of the three lowest Sefiroth, Netzach-Victory, Hod-Splendor, and Yesod-Foundation, into Malkuth-Kingship. In the

---

[32] (Kaplan 1979, 169)

diagram of Thirty-two Paths, Shin is the channel between Hod-Splendor and Netzach-Victory...'[33]

This would, of course, leave the third Mother letter Mem, as the being placed on the path between Chesed and Din in the center of the Sefiroth.

However, according to the *Sefer Yetzirah* 3:6, each of the three Mother letters represents an element that corresponds to where that element is found in the body.

'*Three Mothers Alef Mem Shin*

in the Soul, male and female,

are the head, belly, and chest.

The head is created from fire,

The belly is created from water,

and the chest, from breath, decides between them.[34]'

Alef corresponds to the element of air as in the Hebrew word for air: AViR, and thus finds a natural home in the lungs that would be located on the Sefiroth map of the body between Chesed and Din. Mem corresponds to the element of water as in the Hebrew word water: MaYiM and thus finds its natural home in the stomach and womb areas that would be located on the Sefiroth map of the body between Netzach and Din. This leaves Shin that corresponds to the element of Fire as in the Hebrew word ESH. This would symbolically represent the fire of creative thought and thus find its natural home on the Sefiroth map between Hochmah and Binah.

---

[33] (Kaplan 1979, 170)
[34] (Kaplan 1990, 150)

This placement of the three mother letters is used by the ARI and the GRA on their diagrams of the Sefiroth. In the end, the Rabbis of the Kabbalah tradition henceforth use this system of the ARI and the GRA. It is for this reason that I will in my Qabalah system base it on logic as presented in the *Sefer Yetzirah* text and therefore I will continue to use what I can of the logic used by the GRA.

Next, we have to examine the seven Double letters. The GRA chose a system different than ARI.   The GRA's system is more readily understandable to our Western thinking so I will examine it. I believe the GRA referred to a specific passage in the *Sefer Yetzirah* for the Mother letters I believe he uses 4:4 to decide how to assign the Double letters.

> *Seven Doubles BGD KPRT,*
> *up and down,*
> *east and west*
> *north and south*
> *and the Holy Palace precisely in the center and it supports them*
> *all.*[35]

I believe he starts with the uppermost sefirah, Keter, and places the first Hebrew letter, Beth, with that vertical path. Then he goes to Hochmah, Binah, Chesed, Din, Tifereth, and ends at Yesod and places each of the letters

---

[35] (Kaplan 1990, 163)

on the path under each of those sefirahs, following a basic up to down and right/east to left/west pattern.

This is the pattern I use and that the GRA used.

However, ARI ends up in a different place. At first, I did not understand the how's and why's of this placement. I had not owned and read any texts of Chaim Vital, the disciple of ARI. When I mentioned my problem to my friend Karen Enfield, who is much more knowledgeable of the TaNaK than I, she after some thought realized that ARI's system seems to reference how the 12 tribes travel in the wilderness and their encampment. Thus, the compass directions are laid out in a specific manner with the paths and the sefirahs of the Tree as ARI envisions it. With her careful explanation, I tried to back this up with my guesswork as confirmation.

I believe the ARI begins with *Sefer Yetzirah* 4:2

Seven Doubles BGD KPRT
Their foundation is
Wisdom, Wealth, Seed,
Life, Dominance, Peace and Grace.[36]

---

[36] (Kaplan 1990, 162)

ARI then seems to associates those seven attributes with the lower

seven sefirahs of Chesed, Din, Tifereth, Netzach, Hod, Yesod, and Malkuth.

I imagine, he also then considered verse *Sefer Yetzirah* 4:4[37] as significant and

starts with the uppermost and the easternmost sefirah that he would

consider as being Chesed. Then he goes to Din in the Northwest, then

Tifereth, then Netzach in the south, then Hod in the west then ending with

Yesod and Malkuth. ARI places the Hebrew letter path on the path going up

from Chesed as Beth, the next path going up from Tifereth is where he places

Dalet, and so on with the last letter Tav going on the upper path off of

Malkuth.

This leaves us with the twelve Elemental letters and the GRA again

chooses a placement different from ARI with these letters.

The GRA recognizes that the twelve letters should be associated

with the twelve diagonal paths of the Tree. The Fifth Chapter of the *Sefer*

Yetzirah lists the twelve birthplaces in the natural order of the alphabet: Heh,

Vav, Zayin, Chet, Tet, Yod, Lamed, Nun, Samekh, Eyin, Tzadi, and Kuf.

Again the top to down, left to right pattern is followed. I believe that since

creation begins with Light, as noted in *Bereshith (Genesis)* 1:1, and the Sun

---

[37] (Kaplan 1990, 163)

rises in the East, that this is the starting point of the compass pattern, going

to South, West, North, and then back to East. *'Whenever you turn, turn toward*

the right (Tractate *Yoma* of the *Talmud* 16b).[38]'

For the GRA he starts with the uppermost Sefirah Keter and places

Heh on the path to the right, and places Vav off of the path to the left. Then

he keeps going on the diagonal paths right to left and down the Tree back

and forth, till he ends with the right path connecting to Malkuth with Tzadi

and then to the left path connecting to Malkuth is where Kuf is placed.

I follow this same pattern.

Now, let me try to follow ARI's logic. ARI I believe focuses on *Sefer*

Yetzirah 5:2.

> *Twelve Elementals*
> *H V Z Ch T Y L N S Eyin TZ K*
> *Their foundations is the twelve diagonal boundaries*
> *The east upper boundary*
> *The east northern boundary,*
> *The east lower boundary,*
> *The south upper boundary,*
> *The south eastern boundary,*
> *The south lower boundary,*
> *The west upper boundary*
> *The west southern boundary*
> *The west lower boundary*
> *The north upper boundary*
> *The north western boundary*

---

[38] (Kaplan 1990, 203)

The north lower boundary,
They extend continually until eternity of eternities and it is they
that are the boundaries of the [Olam] Universe.[39]

Continuing with the insights offered by Ms. Enfield, this would make the east as being the path between Keter and Hochmah, south as being at Chesed, the west as being the path between Yesod and Hod, and lastly north as being Binah.

ARI places Heh as the East upper boundary on the path between Keter and Hochmah. He places the South upper boundary with the letter Chet on the path between Chesed and Tifereth. He places the west upper boundary with the letter Lamed on the path between Yesod and Hod. He places the north upper boundary with the letter Eyin on the path between Binah and Tifereth.

He places the east northern boundary with the letter Vav on the path closest to the north area on the path between Keter and Binah. He places the south-eastern boundary with the letter Tet on the path closest to the south area on the path between Hochmah and Tifereth. He places the west southern boundary with the letter Nun on the path closest to the south area on the path between Netzach and Yesod. He places the northwestern

---

[39] (Kaplan 1990, 203)

boundary with the letter Tzadi on the path closest to the west area on the path between Din and Tifereth.

This leaves the east lower boundary and the letter Zayin on the path between Hochmah and Din; the south lower boundary and the letter Yod on the path between Netzach and Tifereth; the west lower boundary and the letter Samekh on the path between Hod and Tifereth; and lastly the north lower boundary and the letter Kuf on the path between Binah and Chesed.

In review, the GRA agrees with ARI on nine letter placements, they are the three Mother letters of Alef, Mem, and Shin, and then the letters Heh, Vav, Chet, Peh, Resh, and Tav. The GRA disagrees with ARI on thirteen letter placements, they are Bet, Gimmel, Dalet, Chet, Tet, Yod, Zayin, Lamed, Nun, Samekh, Eyin, Tzadi, and Kuf.

However, the logic that ARI uses is so immersed in his understanding of Torah and Rabbinic Judaism that I believe that it is too difficult to be used to build a non-Jewish system upon it. Rather I suggest the GRA's simple logic which seems to be purposely built upon a simple reading of the *Sefer Yetzirah* does offer a way for us to explore the Occult. Therefore, I will use the GRA's placement of the letters and his array of the Tree. The difference between the GRA's Tree and the Zohar/Ari Tree is four lines; the GRA has a path connecting Binah to Daat and Daat to Chesed, and

a path connecting Hochmah to Daat and Daat to Din.

'The 32 Paths of Wisdom'

Many copies of the *Sefer Yetzirah* often have an additional later text appended to it. This text is the *Thirty-two Paths of Wisdom*. This text is a list of descriptions for each of the thirty-two paths. It is clear to the Rabbis and the Qabalists that the number 32 is taken from the fact that there are 10 sefirahs and 22 paths connecting them on the Sefiroth. It is clear that each one of the descriptions refers to one of the ten and then each letter/path. All we need to do is decide how to assign the descriptions to those sefirahs and the paths.

It all seems like a simple task. When you compare the two sets of assignments the differences between the two are glaring. There exists a mess of misunderstandings. Out of the 32 listed names, the two groups only make the same choices three times.

The logic of the Qabalists appears to be the following.

"Now, it would seem logical that this text is a list of descriptive attributes of each of the paths on the Sefiroth. It would seem that these attributes were meant to further define and describe the 32 constituent parts of the Sefiroth. If this is the case then how do you assign the attributes to the Sefiroth? Obviously, the first 10 attributes were the most important, and they must be placed at the top of the list. What are the 10 most important parts of the Tree of Life? Why, the 10 sefirahs, of course. Hence, the first attribute on the list must describe the first, the top most sefirah: Keter. The next attribute is describing the next sefirah counting down from the top and so on. The next 22 attributes are assigned to the 22 paths. The 22 paths are numbered by the letters of the Hebrew alphabet. The first letter is Alef so the 11th attribute must be describing the Alef path, the second letter in Hebrew is bet, thus this must be the 12th attribute, and so on till the 32nd attribute is assigned to the last letter of the Hebrew alphabet Tav. Perfectly logical." At least that is what the Qabalists believe.

Here is Dion Fortune describing exactly what I had just explained.

This Tree, Otz Chiim, consists of the Ten Holy Sephiroth arranged in a particular pattern and connect by lines, which are called the Thirty-two Paths of the Sepher Yetzirah, *or Divine Emanations (see The* Sepher Yetzirah, *by Wynn Westcott). Here there exists one of the "blinds", or traps for the uninitiated, in which the ancient Rabbis delighted. We find if we count them, that there are twenty-two, not thirty-two Paths upon the Tree; but for their purpose the Rabbis treated the Ten Sepiroth themselves as Paths, thus misleading the uninitiated. Thus the first ten Paths of the* Sepher Yetzirah *are assigned to the Ten Sephiroth, and the following twenty-two to the actual Paths themselves. It will then be seen how the twenty-two letters of the Hebrew alphabet can be associated with the paths without discrepancy or overlapping.*[40]

---

[40] (Fortune 1935, 23)

Let's note a few things here. One she says she has read Westcott's English translation of the *Sefer Yetzirah*. Two, she says she uses this text to gain insight into her understanding of the Tree. Three, she assumes that the text the *Thirty-two Paths of Wisdom* is assigned exactly as I described, first to the sefirahs and then to the alphabet. If she actually learned anything from what she read she would have seen that the *Sefer Yetzirah* text describes over and over the 3, 7, 12 patterns, and if she really did count and think at the same time the paths on the Tree she would have found the same 3, 7,12 pattern. However, it seems was too difficult a task for her. Instead, she keeps Kircher's letter assignment. She does assign the appellations from the *Thirty-two Paths of Wisdom* by that simplistic method.

However, the Rabbis were not thinking like a Westerner. The game of Kabbalah is based on rabbinic Judaism's first premise that everything of importance is to be found by making reference to the *Torah* and then the commentaries to the *Torah*. Now *Torah* can mean the literal first five books of the *Hebrew Scriptures*, or it can be a term that is expanded to cover all of the *TaNaK*.

So, here is how the rabbis play the game.

"So, what are we to do with this book the *32 Paths of Wisdom*? How are we to assign this to the Sefiroth? Since, the Sefiroth represents not only the structure of the Divine but also, all of creation and the things created as well. So, let us look at the account of creations in the first book of Torah, Bereshith (aka Genesis). Well look at this, In the Hebrew text, the first chapter of Bereshith consists of thirty-two verses describing the acts of creation. Thirty-two is the exact number of the 10 Sefiroth and its 22 paths; this must be the Holy One Blessed Be He trying to give us the key. Now, let's see if we can use these verses as the key to assigning the attributes. Look at this; in those thirty-two verses, there were ten times that the verse mentions HaShem[41] *creating* something. There were three times when HaShem *made* something. There were 7 times that HaShem said *a thing was good*. Once you subtract out the 10+3+7 verses you have a remaining number of 12 verses where nothing new is creating but what has been created is only talked about. Ah-ha! This sequence of 10, 3, 7, and 12 matches the 10 sefirahs and the 3 Mother letters of the Hebrew alphabet, the 7 Double letters of the Hebrew alphabet, and the remaining 12 Elemental letters. Now we have the key to assigning the list of 32 attributes." Now that is how the Rabbis play the game of Kabbalah, a very different way than those Qabalists.

---

[41] HaShem is Hebrew for 'The Name' and is used to refer to the Holy One Blessed Be He, aka God.

According to their system of logic, the 32 verses lay out this way

using those verses from the first chapter of Genesis.

1:God created *the heaven and the earth*=1st *sefirah Keter*

2: =1st *elemental Heh*

3:God said *[when God says something this is treated as an act of creation by the Rabbis], let there be light*=2nd *sefirah Hochmah*

4: God saw the light that it was good=1st *Double Bet*

5:=2nd *elemental Vav*

6:=3rd *elemental Zayin*

7:God said *[created], let there be a firmament*=3rd *sefirah Binah*

8:God made *the firmament*=1st *Mother Alef*

9:=4th *elemental Chet*

10:God said *[created], let the waters be gathered*=4th *sefirah Chesed*

11:=5th *elemental Tet*

12:God saw that it was good=2nd *Double Gimmel*

13:God said *[created], let the earth be vegetated*=5th *sefirah Din*

14:God saw that it was good=3rd *Double Dalet*

15:God said *[created], let there be luminaries*=6th *sefirah Tifereth*

16: God made *two luminaries*=2nd *Mother Mem*

17:=6th *elemental Yod*

18:God saw that it was good=4th *Double Kaf*

19:God said *[created] let the waters swarm*=7th *sefirah Netzach*

20: =7th *elemental Lamed*

21:God saw that it was good=5th *Double Peh*

22:=8th *Elemental Nun*

23:God said *[created] let the earth bring forth animals*=8th *sefirah Hod*

24:God made *the beasts of the field*=3rd *Mother Shin*

25:God saw that it was good=6th *Double Resh*

26:God said *[created], let us make man*=9th *sefirah Yesod*

27:=9th *Elemental Samekh*

28:=10th *Elemental Ayin*

29:=11th *Elemental Tzadi*

30:God said *[created], be fruitful and multiply*=10th *sefirah Malkuth*

31:=12th *Elemental Kuf*

32:God saw all that He had made...called it very good=7th Double Tav[42]

The Kabbalist's logic makes sense to the Kabbalists. However, the Occult Qabalists never dreamed of such a system because they were not living and thinking in the rabbinic worldview of the Kabbalah.

I will list the names of each of the paths from the *Thirty-two Paths of Wisdom* as they are listed by Westcott's translation from Latin. Then, I will give the name using Kaplan's English translation of the original Hebrew text and put it in these brackets ( ). Lastly, I will mark each according to the system being used K [Kabbalah] and Q [Qabalah].

1) Admirable or Concealed Intelligence (Mystical Consciousness) K=Keter Q= Keter

2) Illuminating Intelligence and is the splendor of the Unity (Radiant Consciousness) K=Heh Q= Hochmah

3) Sanctifying Intelligence (Sanctified Consciousness) K=Hochmah Q=Binah

4) Measuring, Cohesive or Receptacular (Settled Consciousness) K=Beth Q=Chesed

---

[42] (Kaplan 1990, 5-7)

5) Radical Intelligence (Rooted Consciousness) K=Vav Q=Din

6) Intelligence of the Mediating Influence (Transcendental Influx Consciousness) K=Zayin Q=Tifereth

7) Occult [as in hidden] Intelligence (Hidden Consciousness) K=Binah Q=Netzach

8) Absolute or Perfect Intelligence (Perfect Consciousness) K=Alef Q=Hod

9) Pure Intelligence (Pure Consciousness) K=Chet Q=Yesod

10) Resplendent Intelligence (Scintillating Consciousness) K=Chesed Q=Malkuth

11) Scintillating Intelligence (Glaring Consciousness) K=Tet Q=Alef

12) Intelligence of Transparency (Glowing Consciousness) K=Gimmel Q=Bet

13) Uniting Intelligence (Unity Directing Consciousness) K=Din Q=Gimmel

14) Illuminating Intelligence (Illuminating Consciousness) K=Dalet Q=Dalet

15) Constituting Intelligence (Stabilizing Consciousness) K=Tifereth Q=Heh

16) Triumphal or Eternal Intelligence (Enduring Consciousness) K=Mem Q=Vav

17) Disposing Intelligence (Consciousness of the Senses) K=Yod Q=Zayin

18) House of Influence (Consciousness of the House of Influx) K=Kaf Q=Chet

19) Intelligence of all the activities of the spiritual beings (Consciousness of the mystery of all spiritual activities) K=Netzach Q=Tet

20) Intelligence of Will (Consciousness of Will) K=Lamed Q=Yod

21) Intelligence of Conciliation (Desired and Sought Consciousness) K=Peh Q=Kaf

22) Faithful Intelligence (Faithful Consciousness) K=Nun Q=Lamed

23) Stable Intelligence (Sustaining Consciousness) K=Hod Q=Mem

24) Imaginative Intelligence (Apparitive Consciousness) K=Shin Q=Nun

25) Intelligence of Probation (Testing Consciousness) K=Resh Q=Samekh

26) Renovating Intelligence (Renewing Consciousness) K=Yesod Q=Eyin

27) Exciting Intelligence (Palpable Consciousness) K= Samekh Q=Peh

28) Natural Intelligence (Natural Consciousness) K=Ayin Q=Tzadi

29) Corporeal Intelligence (Physical Consciousness) K= Tzadi Q=Kuf

30) Collecting Intelligence (General Consciousness) K=Malkuth Q=Resh

31) Perpetual Intelligence (Continuing Consciousness) K= Kuf Q=Shin

32) Administrative Intelligence (Worshipped Consciousness) K=Tav Q=Tav

The Qabalah and The Tarot

The History of the Tarot is a subject of many fanciful legends made up by many 'masters of Occult knowledge' to impress their readers/listeners. Some sources for the historical background of the Tarot are the excellent *Dictionary of the Tarot* by Bill Butler or the three volumes of the 1990 *Encyclopedia of the Tarot* by Stuart Kaplan. Or Sandra A. Thomson's *Pictures from the Heart: A Tarot Dictionary*. Or Robert Place's 2005 book *The Tarot: History, Symbolism, and Divination*. One can even reference Arthur Edward Waite's book *The Pictorial Key to the Tarot* published in 1910. He gives an excellent account of the true and false origins of the Tarot.

In reality, the origin of the Tarot is European. The earliest decks of French and Italian origin date from around 1420s, and around 1530, those cards were made to be used in the card game Tarocchi.

The first Tarot deck designed and specifically crafted as an Occult divination tool was invented by Etellie in the year 1788.[43] This deck followed those early French and Italian decks in style and form with some modifications. Etellie's deck and all subsequent Tarot decks included what is called the Major Arcana collection of cards and also what is called the

---

[43] (Revak 2001)

Minor Arcana cards. The Minor Arcana collection resembled an ordinary playing card deck with four suits numbered one through ten, and then a set of court cards, a king, a queen, and rather than the last court card being the Jack, here is where Etellie's deck and all other Tarot decks differ, there were two other court cards, he had a page and a knight. Etellie's deck and all other Tarot decks had rather than the playing cards suits of Clubs, Diamonds, Hearts and Spades, his Tarot Deck had Cups, Pentacles, Swords, and Wands. The Minor Arcana cards images being depictions of a collection of suits images in accordance with the card's number. The Major Arcana collection of the deck had pictures of symbolic and metaphoric beings; there were twenty-two of these cards.

The next Tarot decks to be invented were made in 1889 by Oswald Wirth. He recounts in his book *Le Tarot, des Imagiers du Moyen Age: The Tarot, the images of the Middle Ages* (published in English in 1985 under the title *The Tarot of the Magicians*.) that under the instructions of Stanislas de Guaita, who studied under Eliphas Levi, Wirth created his own deck of the 22 Major Arcana, based upon these earlier French and Italian decks. Papus used Wirth's deck in his own 1889 book *Le Tarot des Bohemiens*.

A significant change in the Tarot occurred when Arthur Edward Waite and the artist Pamela Coleman-Smith created their deck in 1910. They changed forever how the Tarot would be depicted. Henceforth all subsequent decks can be described as variations of Waite and Smith's deck or variations of the pre-Waite and Smith decks. The innovation of Waite and Smith in their 1910 Tarot created for the first time pictorial and allegorical images to be associated with the Minor Arcana suit cards of the deck. This deck also renumbered the Major Arcana. All subsequent decks that have a pictorial/allegorical imagery rather than merely showing a collection of rods/wands, cups, swords, and pentacles, follow in the footsteps of Smith and Waite.

Now let me trace the connection of the Tarot to the Qabalah. The tale of this connection starts with the publishing of Antoine Court de Gebelin's (1719? - 1784) nine-volume set *Le Monde Primitif Analyse et Compare avec le Monde Moderne,* published in Paris in 1782. In volume eight there was presented the fanciful and false idea that the Tarot was of Egyptian origin. This was in the essay by Louis-Raphael-Lucrece de Fayolle, le Comte de Mellet (1727-1804). Le Comte de Mellet also begins to present in that essay the idea that the Tarot's Major Arcana can be linked to the letters of the Hebrew alphabet. He does this in a curious way. De Mellet only assigns the letter Tav, the last Hebrew letter, to the Fool, which was the last of the cards he discusses. In this essay, de Mellet had been discussing each of the cards of the Major Arcana starting with card 21 The World, and working backward towards card 1 the Magician, and then card 0 the Fool. *'It is logical to assume that he would have assigned the first letter, Alef, to the World, and proceeded through the alphabet assigning the letters in that reverse direction.'*[44] Why de Mellet failed to continue the assigning of the letters to the cards in his essay is a puzzle without an answer.

Presumably, de Mellet recognized the following facts:

1) There are 22 letters in the Hebrew alphabet.

2) There are 22 cards that make up the Tarot's Major Arcana.

We had to wait till Eliphas Levi for someone to assign fully the Hebrew letters to the Tarot deck's Major Arcana. Eliphas Levi was inspired by Court de Gebelin's books[45]. These facts were synergistically connected by Levi and became a matter of Qabalah dogma ever since the publication of Levi's first book in 1854: *Dogma et Rituel de la Haute Magie: The Dogma and Rituals of High Magic*. This connection is further elucidated and filled out in Levi's 1861 book: *La Clef des Grands Mysteres*:

Levi continues the connection of the Tarot to the Hebrew letters and states that each of the Major Arcana cards is associated with a letter of the

---

[44] (Place 2005, 40)
[45] (Place 2005, 38-40)

Hebrew alphabet. Levi went to the natural order of the Tarot's Major Arcana. Levi and Wirth following Levi did the same. Levi linked the ten sefirahs to the Minor Arcana cards, Keter assigned to card one, and so on with Malkuth assigned to card ten.

Eliphas Levi begins his assignment his own way and does not resort to Count de Mellet's idea of starting with the World. Levi begins at the beginning with the first card the Magician that is assigned the number one and the first letter of the Hebrew alphabet, Alef, and so on. However, Levi does a curious thing, when it comes to the card The Fool. He assigns it the number zero but puts it into a place in the order that is odd to me, though obviously made sense to Levi. This assignment is taken up by those who studied and came after Levi, Oswald Wirth, and Papus. Here is what Levi does:

The Sun is marked as 19 and associated with the letter Kuf, the 19th letter in the Hebrew alphabet.

Judgment is marked as 20 and associated with the letter Resh, the 20th letter in the Hebrew alphabet.

The Fool is marked as 0 and associated with the letter Shin, which is the 21st letter in the Hebrew alphabet.

The World is marked as 21 and associated with the letter Tav, which

is the 22nd letter in the Hebrew alphabet.[46]

Robert Place explains that '*Levi's theory of correspondence between the*

trumps and the Hebrew alphabet is based on the idea that the order of the trumps as

found in the Tarot of Marseilles is the original order...Even in the Tarot of

Marseilles, there are not actually twenty-two trumps, but only twenty-one, which

are numbered and considered to be a unified group. The Fool is an extra wild card.[47]'

In that deck the Fool is unnumbered.

Now Levi makes mention of the *Sefer Yetzirah* in his book, so he

could have possibly read it, though I do not believe he did in the original

Hebrew, but rather in a more readily available translation. However, Levi

makes no formal overt connection to the Sefiroth with its twenty-two paths

and the Tarot's Major Arcana and those twenty-two cards.

It is because of Levi's writings and the impact they had on those

who came after him, that the Tarot came to be associated with the Kabbalah

and thus the creation of the Qabalah. However, there exists no reference to

the Tarot in the Kabbalah literature. I have searched *The Bahir, The Sefer*

Yetzirah, The Zohar, the index to the English edition of the *Talmud*, and all the

---

[46] (Levi, Transcendental Magic its Doctrine and Ritual 1896, 133-138)
[47] (Place 2005, 73)

commentaries of *Torah* and collections of Hebrew Midrashim [collections of tales and legends] that I could find. No mention is made in all of that material of the Tarot.

Now it appears that the next important step in the history of the connection between the Qabalah and the Tarot I believe comes out of the Golden Dawn organization around 1900 and I assume it is through the work of Samuel Liddell MacGregor Mathers. In 1888 he writes a short work on the Tarot. In this work, he assigns the Hebrew letters to Major Arcana. There appears to be evidence from the Book *The Magical Tarot of the Golden Dawn*, by Pat and Chris Zalewski, that Robert Felkin and Wynn Westcott took Mathers's work as a starting point and further worked on creating the beginnings of a more formal deck. Nevertheless, Mathers had worked out an assignment of the Major Arcana and the Hebrew letters.

This pattern is the following[48]

Fool 0 Alef

Magician 1 Bet

High Priestess 2 Gimmel

Empress 3 Dalet

---

[48] (Gurney 2009)

Emperor 4 Heh

Hierophant 5 Vav

Lovers 6 Zayin

Chariot 7 Chet

Strength 8 Tet

Hermit 9 Yod

Wheel of Fortune 10 Kaf

Justice 11 Lamed

Hanged Man 12 Mem

Death 13 Nun

Temperance 14 Samekh

The Devil 15 Eyin

The Tower 16 Peh

The Star 17 Tzadi

The Moon 18 Kuf

The Sun 19 Resh

Judgment 20 Shin

The World 21 Tav

The Golden Dawn uses the associations of the Hebrew letters, and thus the Major Arcana, to be mapped unto the Sefiroth using Kircher's Array.

Now in 1910 When Arthur Edward Waite and Pamela Coleman-Smith created their Tarot deck although what they did not do was associate Hebrew letters with the Major Arcana. Waite in his Tarot deck switched the position of the cards Justice and Strength.

The next important player in the game of connecting the Tarot to the Qabalah was Aleister Crowley. He had translated and published Eliphas Levi's *The Key to the Great Mysteries* in Equinox volume Ten in the fall of 1913. Crowley repeats the connection of the Hebrew alphabet to the Tarot in his own writings. He switches the Fool's position in the Major Arcana and how the Fool corresponds to the Hebrew alphabet to something other than how Levi sets it out. In 1904 in a burst of inspiration Crowley transcribes his book *Liber Al vel Legis, sub figura CCXX, The Book of the Law*. It was a poetic and cryptic masterpiece of Occult wisdom.

In 1909 the first version of *Liber 777* is published[49]. Crowley notes in his vast collection of charts from *Liber 777* that the letters of the Hebrew

---

[49] (Crowley, Liber 777 And Other Qabalistic Writings of Aleister Crowley Including Gematria & Sepher Sephiroth 1907, 1909, 1947, 1973, iii)

alphabet correspond to the cards of the Major Arcana and these both further correspond to the 22 paths found on the Sefiroth.

Crowley eventually realized in a manner similar to the Rabbis, that a *Written Torah* needs an *Oral Torah*; hence, there must be commentaries to his own text. Crowley begins his first set of commentaries to his *Book of Law* in 1912. However, he was still not satisfied and so his second set of commentaries is completed in 1921. In the 1921 comments to Section II:8 of *The Book of Law*, Crowley states that Hoor-Paar-Kraat or Harpocrates: *'He is the First Letter of the Alphabet, Alef, whose number is One, and his card in the Tarot is The Fool, numbered zero.'*[50]

Again for Crowley, the links of Tarot and Qabalah are the same. The image of the Sefiroth that Crowley uses is Kircher's Tree as illustrated on page xxvii of *Liber 777*. Crowley further explored the Tarot and its relation to the Sefiroth when he set out to create his own Tarot deck. This deck began in 1938 and continued to completion in 1943, and was published in private circulation as *The Book of Thoth* in 1944. In the material associated with this deck, Crowley described his theory of the Tarot. This deck was first publically made available through The O.T.O. in 1969.

---

[50] (Crowley, The New and Old Commentaries to Liber Al vel Legis, The Book of the Law by Aliester Crowley 1996)

Crowley makes note of, as Levi put it, of Hebrew Grammar. *'They [The 22 Major Arcana cards] are attributed as follows: the three Mother letters, Shin, Mem and Alef, represent the three active elements, the seven so-called double letters, Beth, Gimmel, Dalet, Kaph, Peh, Resh, and Tav, represent the seven sacred planets. The remaining twelve letters, Heh, Van, Zayin, Cheth, Teth, Yod, Lamed, Nun, Samekh, A'ain, Tzadi, and Qoph, represent the Signs of the Zodiac.'*[51]

Despite this recognition and acknowledgment of the importance of the *Sefer Yetzirah's* logic, Crowley uses for his illustration of the Tree with its paths in a manner as numbered by the Christian Cabalist Kircher.

Kircher had used a simple top-down, right to left placement of the letters starting with Alef and just going down the alphabet sequence. The trouble with this is that Kircher has no understanding or no appreciation of, as Levi puts it, the grammar of the Hebrew alphabet. Kircher's diagram of the Tree with his letter placement appears in his book *Oedipus Aegyptiacus,* published in 1652-1654. In that text is a translation of the Sefer Yetzirah. However, either Kircher didn't do the translation; or he did, and did not learn anything from it, or being a Jesuit did not care to acknowledge that the

---

[51] Crowley, *Book of Thoth,* section 'The Twenty-Two Keys, ATU, or Trumps of the Tarot', pg. 14, taken from the internet website: http://www.private.org.il/GD/Book_of_Thoth.pdf.

Jews were of any value and thus deliberately ignored the *Sefer Yetzirah* when he created his diagram of the Tree.

Kircher ignores the correspondence of the horizontal, diagonal, and vertical lines and how they correspond to the 3, 7, 12 groupings of the Hebrew letters. Thus, Kircher creates his own placement of the Hebrew letters on the 22 paths. Kircher begins with the first sefirah, Keter, and notes that there are three lines coming out of it and thus assigns the first three letters of the Hebrew alphabet to them going left to right and top to bottom. He continues around to Binah filling in the paths with the next letters of the alphabet and so on down through the Tree.

Kircher's placement is the frustration of Crowley: '*Twenty-two is the number of the letters of the Hebrew alphabet. It is the number of the Paths of the Sepher Yetzirah. These paths are the paths which join the ten numbers [the sefirahs] on the figure called the Tree of Life. Why are there twenty-two of them? Because that is the number of the letters of the Hebrew alphabet and one letter goes to each path. Why should this be so? Why should these paths be arranged on the Tree in the way that the diagram* [referring to Kircher's diagram of the Tree] *shows? Why should there not be paths connecting the numbers 2 [Chakmah] and 5 [Din] and the numbers 3 [Binah] and 4 [Chesed]? One cannot answer any of these*

questions.'[52]

Crowley's frustration is evident. Crowley's genius failed him in this

instance. He was not able to ignore the Jesuit Christian Kircher and his old

book. I speculate that this is due to Crowley's own unconscious Christian

cultural bias and how it would not let him challenge the Kircher's authority

given the antiquity of the text. He simply assumed that old must equal true.

A foolish mistake.

Now, there are two parts to resolving Crowley's frustration with the

Kircher picture. One is to go back to the Kabbalah source material and find

the array used by the Kabbalists. This array has a path connecting Hochmah

to Din and Binah to Chesed. I believe that Crowley is also frustrated in his

understanding of the Sefiroth because he does not recognize the array

version that Kircher was using was different than the one from *Sha'are Orah*

and *The Zohar*, see Figure 2 and 8. Kircher ignored how the rabbis described

the letters in the *Sefer Yetzirah* and thus how to place the Hebrew letters on

the Sefiroth. Kircher's failure is Crowley's frustration. As I believe, Crowley

simply assumed that Kircher's very old diagram must be true and correct

---

[52] (Crowley, The Book of Thoth from Equinox volume 3 no. 5 1998,
35-36)

on the basis of its age alone. Crowley not being Jewish did not appreciate the logic of Hebrew as explained in the *Sefer Yetzirah* and failed to accept that a Jew's logic would be true when it challenges a Christian Jesuits. The fact that the *Sefer Yetzirah* and all of the Kabballah were created by Jewish rabbis was totally ignored and dismissed by Crowley. He accepted the dogma of Christianity that devalues the teachings and beliefs of the Jews and that they were supplanted by Christianity.

In any case, Crowley followed Kircher and used an un-Kabbalistic matching of letters to the paths on the Tree.

Now Crowley's placement of the Major Arcana of the Tarot on the Tree is based on how he associates each of the 22 Major Arcana cards with the Hebrew letters. Crowley does so with a system of his own devising based on his vision and channeling of the *Book of the Law*, and how he believes the cards are associated with the Hebrew letters, the Zodiac, and Astrology. Crowley switches the Hebrew letters associated with the Emperor and the Star, making the Star associated with the Hebrew letter Heh and the Emperor associated with the Hebrew letter Tzadi. Although Crowley does not alter those two cards' numerical sequence, thus the Emperor is still card number IV and the Star is card number XVII. I am not a master of Crowley's texts and the Thelema tradition he created and inspired and therefore I am not going down this path any further.

Paul Foster Case, who was once a member of the Golden Dawn, like Crowley, is next in our historical chronology. '*Dr. Case first began the study of the Tarot in 1900 at the age of sixteen. In 1907 he published the attributions of the Tarot Keys to the letters of the Hebrew alphabet set forth in this [The Tarot, a Key to the Wisdom of the Ages] book. In 1920 Dr. Case published An Introduction to the Study of the Tarot, now out of print, which was the precursor to this book.*[53]' Tarot was further discussed in his 1927 book *A Brief Analysis of the Tarot* and again in his 1931 book *Highlights of Tarot*.

In his 1920 book *An Introduction to the Study of the Tarot* Case offers the connection between the paths of the Sefiroth based on Kircher's array and assignment of the Hebrew alphabet to the paths, and through that to the assigning the Major Arcana to the paths. In Chapter Three page 12 of the book Case notes in the footnote that he makes use of Crowley's *Liber 777* 1909 book. Case follows the assignment of The Fool to 0 and the Hebrew letter Alef and places the Fool at the beginning of the deck. Case does keep Arthur Edward Waite's idea of having card number 8 the Strength card and

---

[53] (Case 1947, preface)

card number 11 as Justice. Paul Foster Case also creates what he calls the Cube of Space based upon the *Sefer Yetzirah,* although he never publically publishes this material and only offers it to those who become members of his organization, the Builders of the Adytum, whose beginnings were in 1922. In this diagram of the Cube of Space, and the material describing the symbolism, Case associates the Major Arcana of the Tarot to the *Sefer Yetzirah's* Cube of Space through the connection of the Hebrew letters with the Major Arcana, the key alignment being the assignment of Alef to the Fool.

What is significant for the history of the Qabalah is that the Sefiroth has been linked with the Tarot. The Golden Dawn, Case, and Crowley's use of Kircher forever links Kircher's tree to the Tarot throughout the literature of the Qabalah. The Qabalists use Kircher's Tree and Kircher's placement of the 22 letters on the 22 paths as their guide to then placing the 22 Tarot cards with the resulting confusion that Crowley noted but could not find a way to resolve.

I believe that it is time to respect the ancestors and creators of the Kabbalah and therefore to go back to the Rabbis source text, specifically the *Sefer Yetzirah,* and create a new form of the Qabalah. Therefore, I will use not the Kircher and the Qabalist system but make a new connection of the Tarot to the Sefiroth using the Kabbalist placement of the Hebrew letters.

One last note, when I offer up my diagram of the assignment of the Major Arcana to the paths of the Sefiroth I do not follow Levi, and Wirth getting it from Levi, in making the Fool correspond to the 21st letter of the Hebrew alphabet Shin and has the World correspond to the 22nd letter of the Hebrew alphabet Tav. I am in agreement with The Golden Dawn, Crowley, and Case on this idea, and believe that the Fool is the 0 card and should come at the beginning, making the Fool correspond with the first letter of the Hebrew alphabet Alef.

De Mellet, Levi, the Golden Dawn, Crowley, and Case were very right. It is a fascinating synergistic union. The Qabalah has been nurtured well by the marriage of the Tarot to the Sefiroth. The marriage is a false one if you are solely interested in the study the Jewish Kabbalah. However, the union has become a truth of the Occult Qabalah. I believe it is well worth exploring the Tarot by utilizing this arrangement on the Sefiroth. The Qabalah has been well served by the Occult magicians' inventiveness.

The Paths Between: The GRA's Tree

In order to get to a system of matching the Hebrew letters to the Major Arcana on the Tree of Life and Knowledge, I needed to decide on which pattern of letters to follow. I ultimately utilized the GRA's assignment of letters to the paths of the Sefiroth. I needed to examine his actual tree and demonstrate the logic of his system of placement on that tree. The reason I am doing this is that the GRA's system of assignment of the letters of the paths is the most seemingly 'commonsense' and understandable assignment and fits naturally with the Tree. Once I explained what he did to create his own version of the tree, then I will explain how I transposed his letter placement onto the Zohar-ARI tree. But first I need to explore the GRA's Tree more in-depth and to do this I need to address an error that an important scholar made.

Kaplan's Error: 1884 Sefer Yetzirah of the GRA and The Fiction of the Natural Array.

In 1997, Aryeh Kaplan published a revised paperback edition to his translation with commentary of the Sefer Yetzirah: The Book of Creation. (Samuel Weiser, Inc., Second Edition 1997). This was an important event. It presented a new English translation of the text, a history of the publication with a history of its commentaries, as well as the detailed erudite commentary that Kaplan offered on the text.

In Appendix IV Kaplan presents 'Editions and Commentaries' of the Sefer Yetzirah, pp 319-337. Kaplan's comment on the 1884 edition is [Note emphasis is added]:

> *Warsaw, 1884, The Standard edition in current use. Consists of two sections. The first section contains all commentaries as in Mantua editions, as well as* Otzar HaShem. *The commentary* Chakamoni, *by R. Shabbatai Donello, is printed separately at the end of this section. Second section contains* Pri Yetzchak *and commentary of Gra, with commentary of Ari at the end. Also contains Long Version at the end. This edition contains many typographical errors in the commentaries.*

Then under the list of commentaries, Kaplan lists those of the GRA:

[Emphasis is added.]

> *Eliahu (Ben Shlomo), Gaon of Vilna, "The Gra", 1720-1797. Considered one of the greatest geniuses of all time. Purely Kabbalistic commentary on the Gra Version, which he edited. First published in Grodno, 1806, and contained in subsequent*

editions, most notably that of Warsaw 1884. An edition edited by his disciple R. Moshe Shlomo of Tulchin, and also containing a supercommentary, Toldot Yitzchak, *by R. Yitzchak ben Yehudah Leib Kahanah (q.v.) was published in Jerusalem, 1874, 186 pp.*

It is the 1884 Warsaw edition which has the GRA's commentary that is the focus of much intense interest by Kaplan and it is this text that offers an illustration that should be called 'The GRA's Tree.' Kaplan uses this illustration on the cover of his book and presents it as well as figure 6 on page 31 of his book.

The intent of this article is to understand and explain what is going on in that figure 6. To explain each line and every intersection and determine what they are. I only care to explain what is actually in that figure, I do not care if that seems to violate some traditional view of what the Sefirot aka Tree, is supposed to be like according to the traditional commentary on the Sefer Yetzirah or Kabbalah in general. As I worked out what is in this figure, I can only conclude that what currently is known as 'Tradition' is based on information that does not take into account this figure. If I had access to an English translation of the 1884 GRA edition of the Sefer Yetzirah then and only then could I determine what is the meaning and purpose behind this figure. Then and only then could we know what the Kabbalah meant to the GRA. I can prove that Kaplan's 'Natural Array' though it bears a resemblance to the GRA's tree in figure 6 it diverges from it. I just do not know why. Kaplan does not explain his intention of creating his Natural Array.

This paper is based on a few assumptions.

1)   Figure 6 (see p 156) called the GRA Tree was indeed rendered under some supervision by the GRA. It therefore will assume it represents his intent and his understanding of the Sefer Yetzirah and the Kabbalah. I will assume he is either creating a new Tradition or working within his understanding of the existing Tradition.

2)   I am assuming that each of the Hebrew letters is assigned to one and only one of the 22 paths of the Tree.

3)   I assume that mistakes in printing and drawing are possible and might be difficult to fix. I am assuming that once an imprint block is set up for the book's publication it is too costly to change totally. Therefore, a mistake becomes permanent, and nothing can be removed, though something might be able to be added.

4)   Human beings have an infinite capacity to rationalize anything. I assume that if my logic and analysis are correct then the GRA invented some explanations to justify what I am describing. Therefore,

either the GRA or I, am rationalizing their work. I am willing to accept that

we both are.

With those assumptions as a foundation, let us begin.

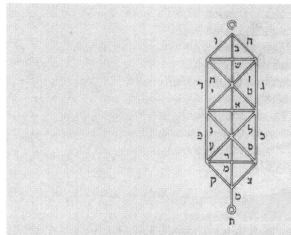

Figure 6. The paths defined by the Gra, as they appear in the Warsaw, 1884 edition, (p. 26b of Part Two).

Figure 6: The GRA's 1884 Tree

Now, a curious thing happened, Aryeh Kaplan created something

he calls the 'Natural Array' found on page 30 of his book, he offers his figure

5 which he labels 'The 32 paths according to the Gra' (see pg 116).

If you do a search on the Internet, you will find images and references to this 'Natural Array' and they all treat it as the 'GRA Tree'. Even though, Kaplan only said this pattern in Figure 5 is 'The Paths according to the Gra', meaning that the letter placement on the paths imitates the pattern that the GRA used for his tree. Though it will turn out that this resemblance is only superficial, as I will explain. Still, the reference 'according to the Gra' associated with Kaplan's Natural Array is I believe the reason that people equate the 'Natural Array' as actually representing the GRA's Tree. I wish to set the record straight and explain that the 'Natural Array' cannot be an accurate representation of the GRA's idea of the tree. This tree in figure 5 is the error I refer to in the title of this article. Kaplan's 'Natural Array' I posit is a fabrication of Kaplan and is a misreading of the GRA's 1884 figure. This article will present my defense of this statement.

It is interesting to note that even Kaplan is a bit dubious about his own 'Natural Array'. The text even says that the 'Natural Array' was never used by the Rabbis. *'In practice, for reasons dealing with the basic nature of the Sefirot, they are not arranged in this natural order but have the middle line lowered somewhat.* '(Kaplan, p. 32)

Kaplan's 'Natural Array', which has become the 'GRA Tree' to many others as evidence by an internet search of that phrase will uncover, is supposedly based on the 1884 illustration from the GRA's text on the Sefer

Yetzirah. I believe that once we carefully examine the 1884 Tree we will see

that you cannot create the 'Natural Array' figure 5 from figure 6 the 1884

GRA Tree.

I will refer to what I will call the ARI Tree as a way to contrast what

is going on in the 1884 GRA tree to a 'standard' Kabbalah Tree image. This

ARI Tree is in Figure 7.

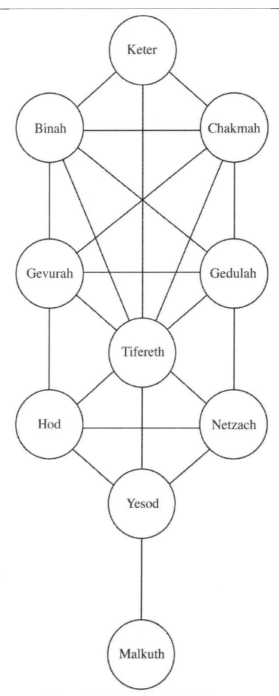

Figure 7: The Zohar / ARI Tree

First, let me explain what I claim is Kaplan's error.

1)   Kaplan states that his Figure 5 is 'The 32 paths according to the Gra.' found on Page 30. Now, this Figure is what Kaplan calls the 'Natural Array'. What others seem to assume is that Figure 5 is an accurate rendering of the GRA's tree figure 6.

2)   If the illustration found in figure 6, is the intended rendering of the GRA's tree then let us compare the two.

3)   At the bottom of Figure 6 is a circle with a line going up to the rest of the design. However, in Kaplan's Figure 5 there is no circle with a line connecting it. Kaplan's Figure 5 is a completely sealed and enclosed design with nothing attached to it. This means that we have to ignore completely that lower circle and the vertical line, which is plainly apparent in the GRA's 1884 figure 6.

4)   This would also mean that the Tav shown below the circle and the mem shown next to the line connecting the circle are both mistakes on the part of the rendering of the GRA's intent.

5)   Kaplan in Figure 5 moves the Tav and Resh letters to appear within this enclosed design. The Tav is being moved to connect what Kaplan calls Malkuth and Yesod. This forces the Resh, which on the GRA's figure 6 clearly shows that it is the line associated with the bottom vertical line.

Kaplan will be pushing that Resh into a new position in his Figure 5. Kaplan has to move Resh to the empty line of the 1884 Figure; this line connects what Kaplan would call Yesod and Tifferet, this is another complete disregard for the depiction of what is shown in his Figure 6.

6)   Kaplan by making Malkuth the lowest sefirah in the central vertical pillar would therefore make the next sefirah above Malkuth, Yesod, and the next one above that Tifferet. This creates new direct relationships between Yesod, Din, and Chesed, which do not exist on the typical ARI tree of my figure 7, as well as disconnecting Tifferet from having a direct relationship with Netzach and Hod, which it does in the typical ARI tree of figure 7. This is evidence of Kaplan creating a completely new array/tree and not rendering a version of either ARI or GRA's tree.

Kaplan has created something completely in violation of what is clearly in his figure 6. He is moving things around, and he is ignoring what is there. This is what I am calling Kaplan's error. Even Kaplan admits that he is doing something outside of the normative tradition, as I quoted before: *'In practice, for reasons dealing with the basic nature of the Sefirot, they are not arranged in this natural order, but have the middle line lowered somewhat.* '(Kaplan, p. 32). Kaplan is referring to the configuration found in the ARI tree, my figure 7.

7)   Therefore, you cannot get from Kaplan's figure 5 from the

GRA's Tree of Figure 6 without those violations, as I am calling them.

8)   It is clear that Kaplan forces the letter arrangement of figure

6 the GRA's 1884 tree onto the paths of his figure 5 and thus refers back to

the work of the GRA. This is not the same as accurately reproducing the

GRA tree as shown in figure 6. Therefore, I concluded that Kaplan's Figure

5 the 'Natural Array' is Kaplan's own invention and not a rendering of the

GRA. I am not dismissing its possible value I am only trying to rectify a

misapprehension associated with that figure. Whoever treats Kaplan's

invented 'Natural Array' as the GRA's Tree is mistaken.

Now I will examine the 1884 GRA Tree Figure 6.

1) On the 1884 GRA Tree Figure 6, there are three horizontal lines.

    On the ARI Tree Figure 7, there are also three horizontal lines.

    These lines on the ARI Tree connect Chokmah and Binah,

    Chesed and Din, and lastly connecting Netzach and Hod.

2) From this, we can assume that the intersections on the GRA

    Tree correspond to connect to those six sefirahs. The letters

    associated and near those lines are Shin, Alef, and Mem.

3) We have now proven that a line with a letter connects to a

    sefirah, which on the GRA Tree figure 6 is designated by an

intersection of lines.

4) When we compare the ARI figure 7 to GRA figure 6, the sefirah above Chokmah and Binah is Keter. That would be the topmost intersection on the GRA figure 6. The diagonal line of Heh connects Keter to Chokmah; the diagonal line of Vav connects Keter to Binah.

5) We know that there are 12 diagonal lines on the Trees and they match the 12 'elemental' Hebrew letters.

6) The circle above Keter on the GRA figure 6 I would assume is Ayn Sof. According to Kabbalah tradition, Ayn Sof is the creator of all and the Tree is a representation of the Divine itself, as well as the blueprint for all created things.

7) There are seven vertical lines on the ARI figure 7 Tree and they would correspond to the vertical lines on the GRA figure 6 Tree. On the GRA Tree, there are 11 vertical lines, if you count each line that connects one intersection with another intersection and you include the line connecting to the lower circle. According to Sefer Yetzirah, the vertical lines match the seven double letters. In the GRA Tree figure 6, we seem to have too many vertical lines. We will consider only the lines that correspond to

one of the Hebrew letters as being real/valid. The easy ones to verify are the Gimel line connecting the intersection we called Chokmah to Chesed; the Dalet line connecting Binah to Din; the Kaf line connecting Chesed to Netzach; and the Peh line connecting Din to Hod.

8) The inner vertical lines are still to be resolved, as well as the inner intersections.

9) What is the circle at the bottom connect to the lowest intersection of the rest of the Tree? This is the key to understanding what is going on in the inner portion of the GRA figure 6 Tree. Near this vertical line is the letter Mem. Below the circle is the letter Tav. The Sefer Yetzirah would tell us that the Mem, one of Mother letters is associated with the three horizontal lines. Therefore[54], the appearance of the Mem near the vertical line seems to be a 'mistake'. The Tav, the last of the double letters should go with the lowest/last vertical line. Let us assume that it does. This assumption would make the circle

---

[54] I am treating Mem as only being one of the 3 mother letters. Any other Kabbalistic tradition beyond that simple reference in the text of the *Sefer Yetzirah* is not being considered here.

Malkuth and the line going to the lowest point/intersection on the Tree, would therefore be Yesod.

10) Therefore, as I said in point #9, I will assume that the lowest circle is Malkuth to be in a parallel special relationship to Ayn Sof. Malkuth is connected to the rest of the Tree, yet not a complete part of it. This will need to be explained.

11) If the circle is Malkuth, and the Tav line connects it to Yesod, this means that the two diagonal lines connecting Yesod to Hod with the Qof line; and connecting Yesod to Netzach with the Tzadi line.

12) Yesod is also connected via the vertical line designated with the Resh to an intersection. This same intersection has 5 lines flowing into it besides the Resh line. They are the Ayin line connecting it to Hod, and the Samek line connecting it to Netzach. This intersection therefore must be Tifferet. Tifferet is also connected to Din by a Nun diagonal line, and the Lamed diagonal line connects it to Chesed.

13) Now we have left with one last intersection on the GRA figure 6. It is where the diagonal Chet line from Binah, the diagonal Zayin line from Chokmah, the diagonal Tet line from Chesed,

the diagonal Yod line from Din, and the vertical Bet line all
converge.

14) Now according to the *Sefer Yetzirah*, there are ten and not eleven
sefirahs. Yet this GRA figure 6 has ten intersecting points with
an additional sefirah as Malkuth represented by the lower
circle. This would seem to violate the rules laid out by the *Sefer
Yetzirah*. Yet, the assumption is that figure 6 was devised by the
GRA himself. He is the Gaon of Vilna, the 'genius of Vilna' and
so we must assume that he is no fool. This figure is attached to
his commentary on the *Sefer Yetzirah*. We therefore must assume
that it was intentional. There must be some reason for ten
intersections and still have Malkuth.

15) My assumption is that Malkuth represented by the circle
connected to Yesod is somehow being treated in this figure as a
different kind of Sefirah. Traditional Kabbalah does designate
Malkuth as completely passive, only reflecting and taking in the
light from all the sefirahs above it. Malkuth is the end product
of creation. Whereas Ayn Sof, also depicted as a circle is The
Creator itself. My leap of faith is that Malkuth is being
considered as somehow outside of the active part of the Tree

and thus not being counted as one of the ten sefirahs, allowing Daat to be counted and shown on the tree. This is solely based on having faith in the genius of the Gaon of Vilna. He, I assumed, created figure 6 and thus he created a visual difference between Malkuth and all the other sefirahs. According to traditional Kabballah, Malkuth is considered a non-active part of the Sefirot. This thereby enables the intersection above Din and Chesed to be a sefirah, and an active sefirah as well. This would make that intersection Daat. I know that according to other traditions of the Kabbalah Daat is not a 'true' sefirah. However, I do not care. I am only concerned with one thing and this is the central point of this paper. I am assuming that the Gaon of Vilna created figure 6 and he intended it to be understood. All I have is the figure, which I believe needs to be understood no matter what. I will stand by my conclusion that figure 6 places a sefirah at the intersection of Bet, Zayin, Tet, Chet, and Yod. Since Tifferet and Malkuth have already been placed on the Tree, this leaves only Daat to be at this intersection.

Leonard R. Glotzer in his book *The Fundamentals of Jewish Mysticism: The Book of Creation and its commentaries*, (1992, Jason Aronson Inc.), offers some insights into the quandary of what is counted as 10 sefirahs.

> *In counting the Sefirot, there have been some debate as to which Sefirot constitutes the ten. The inclusion of three Sefirot—Keter, Daat, and Malchut—has sometimes been questioned. Sefer Yetzirah begins with the Paths of Wisdom. Keter is not explicitly mentioned. It has been called Ayin, nonbeing. Even the Torah itself begins with an allusion to Wisdom rather than Keter. It will be remembered that the phrase "In the beginning" refers to Wisdom, as it says in Proverbs, "The beginning of wisdom" (Proverb 4:7). Daat is often not mentioned in the list of Sefirot. It only appears at times when Keter is neglected. Its status is somewhat elusive. Malchut is the last of the Sefirot. It has no light of its own and is a recipient of the light of the other Sefirot. It is, therefore, compared to the moon, while Zair Anpin is the sun. Since Malchut does not have its own light, perhaps it should not be counted.*[55]*
>
> *Rabbi Moses Cordovero, in Padres Rimonim states, "Ordinary Daat refers to the Sefirah of Tiffert. (Pardes Rimonim, Shaar HaArachim, Daat.)" According to this, Daat is not an eleventh Sefirah. We sometimes find that it is associated with Keter and is considered to be the presence of Keter below. It is the mediating aspect of Keter and helps unite Wisdom and Understanding. Since Tiferet is also a mediator, Daat may be considered either Tiferet above or Keter below. The idea is the same. It resolves the Wisdom-Understanding antithesis.*
>
> *Other explanations have been offered. For instance, it has been said that Daat is not counted because it is always concealed. That is because it serves to unite Chachmah and Binah. The Zohar states that Chachmah and Binah never separate. Therefore, Daat, which is between them, is always concealed in their union. The Sefirah of Yisod serves the same function for Zair Anpin and Malcuth. However, the union of Zair Anpin and Malcuth is only*

[55] This idea is found in Zohar II 145b, Zohar I 249b, 250a.

occasional, so Yisod is not always covered. Therefore, it is counted. (Pree Yitzchak in the name of the Ari, Chapter1, Mishnah 4.)

Another theory offered by the Ari is that Daat does not have its own inner content, but rather holds the light to be passed to the lower Sefirot. Therefore, it is not counted separately when the inner aspect of the Sefirot is counted. Keter is counted instead. However, the opposite is true when counting the outside of the Sefirot. The outside is for the purpose of creation, and creations begins with Wisdom (being). Therefore, Daat is included, but not Keter (Pree Yitzchak in the name of the Ari, Chapter1, Mishnah 4.)

Finally, as far as Malchut is concerned, it is usually counted despite the lack of its own light. It is considered a key Sefirah in that its elevation is a central theme in Kabbalah. However, building on the Lurian model, the Vilna Gaon states that in certain cases, Malchut is not counted. For instance, within the Partzuf of Arich Anpin, two aspects of Keter exist ['upper Keter' sefirah Keter, and the 'lower Keter' = sefirah Daat] and each is counted separately. Malchut, which would be the eleventh Sefirah, is therefore excluded. (Eliyahu Gaon of Vilna, commentary on Sefer Yetzirah, Chapter 1, Mishnah 4, Ofan 1.) [Glotzer, pp21-22 with my own emphasis added.]

In summary, if you exclude either Keter or Malkuth from being considered part of the 10 sefirahs in the tree then you have allowed Daat to be included on the tree. It is not my place to decide which of those explanations is correct. Though, as I just noted in a footnote, that idea of Malkuth not being like the other sefirahs is an idea held in the Zohar. I believe that the later explanation offered by the GRA, as cited by Glotzer and using the ideas found in the Zohar, is what is depicted in the 1884 GRA

Tree figure 6. This is my speculation. Since all I care to do is to state that

Daat appears to be placed on this tree in figure 6 and so is Malkuth as the

circle at the bottom. Which I presume is to visually represent its status as

outside of the 10 other active forces within the Godhead and thus not a full

sefirah of the Sefiroth.

16) Now the only remaining line not described is the line from Daat

to Tifferet. You will note that there is no letter next to it. I deem

this significant. I will assume that the vertical Bet line starts at

Keter, goes through Daat, flows to, and connects to Tifferet.

Thus denoting that Daat has a special relationship on the Tree

as depicted by the GRA.

17) As to how many vertical lines are there on the Figure 6 Tree,

according to the rule, there can only be 7, one associated with

each of the letters, Bet, Gimel, Dalet, Kaf, Peh, Resh, and Tav.

This means that the point found because of the crossing of the

Alef horizontal line between Chesed and Din and the Bet

Vertical line appearing between Keter and Tifferet does not

signify a Sefirah. It also means that the point found because of

the crossing of the Resh line between Tifferet and Yesod and the

Mem line between Netzach and Hod does not signify a Sefirah.

Therefore there are only 7 vertical lines: Bet connecting Keter and Tifferet by passing through Daat, Gimel connecting Chokmah and Chesed, Dalet connecting Binah and Din, Kaf connecting Chesed and Netzach, Peh connecting Din and Hod, Resh connecting Tifferet and Yesod, and Tav connecting Yesod and Malkuth.

I have now taken note of and explained all the lines and intersections on the GRA 1884 Tree as depicted in Figure 6. In conclusion, I offer my drawing of what I believe correctly represents GRA's 1884 tree, as figure 8.

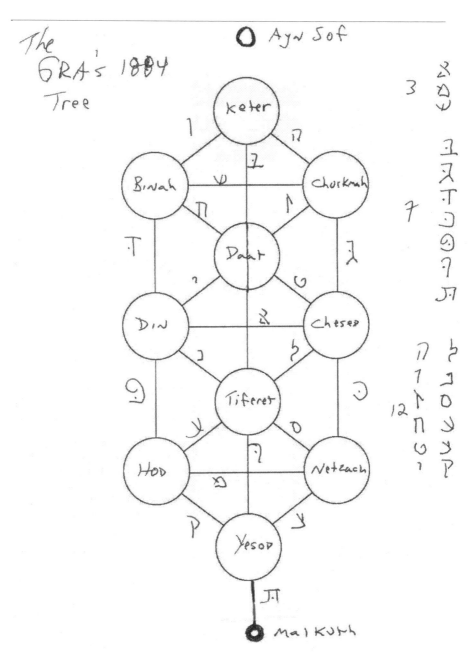

Figure 8: My rendering of the GRA's 1884 Tree

Taking the GRA's Tree letters and placing them on ARI's Tree

Now I wish to assign the letters to Zohar/ARI's Tree. As I have stated before, ARI's Tree, figure 7, is the array most commonly associated with the Jewish Kabballah. The array is built off of the assumption that there must be only one line connecting Yesod to Malkuth.

The difference between the GRA's tree and the ARI's tree is that on the ARI tree the sefirah Daat has faded from the tree, and its influence and effect on the paths and connections between the other sefirahs are not as present as it is on the GRA's tree of 1884. Rendering Malkuth to be considered as part of the ten sefirahs that make up the Sefiroth and therefore Daat is not counted amongst them, as it was in the GRA's tree of 1884.

One theological explanation could be to say the sefirah that shattered was Daat. Another explanation would be to say that when Eve took the fruit off the Tree of Knowledge and Life, it was as if she plucked Daat off the tree, and that is what she and Adam ate. In both of those explanations, the paths would have to shift to acknowledge the absence of Daat.

The four paths that are affected by the presence and absence of Daat on the tree are Zayin, Chet, Tet, and Yod. On the GRA's tree, Zayin went from Hochmah to Daat, Chet went from Binah to Daat, Tet went from Chesed to Daat, and Yod went from Din to Daat.

With the removal of Daat, the paths need to be realigned. To accommodate this realigning I will maintain the path's starting point. Therefore Zayin will start from Hochmah, Chet will start from Binah, Tet will start from Chesed and Yod will start from Din.

Chesed's path of Tet will now connect to Binah going through the place where Daat once was. Din's path of Yod will now connect to Hochmah going through the place where Daat once was. This causes the Zayin and the Chet path to need a new way to travel and connect to a sefirah. The Zayin path will drop down and now connect Hochmah to Tifereth. The Chet path will drop down and now connect Binah to Tifereth.

These shifting paths will now yield the array that is known as the Zohar/ARI tree. What follows is my GRA inspired placement of the Hebrew letters on the Zohar/ARI array of the Tree.

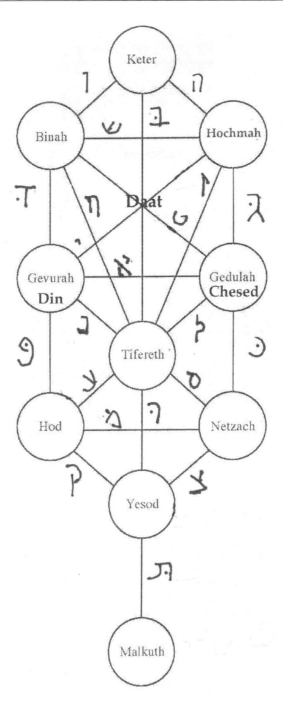

Figure 9: Zohar/ARI Tree with my application of GRA Letters

The Tarot on the ARI Tree with My GRA letters

Now as I said before, we will use my placement of the GRA letters on the ARI array of the Sefiroth. We can now lay out the Tarot major arcana to the paths. This is found in figure 10.

I will append Westcott's / Kaplan's translation of the attributes associated with each letter from the *32 Paths of Wisdom,* as well as the paragraph number from this text.

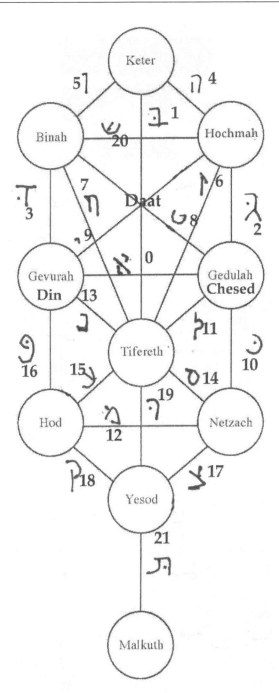

Figure 10: ARI Tree My Letters & Major Arcana Numbers

The Major Arcana assigned with GRA logic to the ARI Array

1) Alef = 0 Fool = Chesed to Din, #8 Absolute or Perfect Intelligence / Perfect Consciousness

2) Beth=1 Magician= Keter to Tifereth, #4 Measuring, Cohesive or Receptacular Intelligence / Settled Consciousness

3) Gimmel = 2 High Priestess=Hochmah to Chesed, #12 Intelligence of Transparency / Glowing Consciousness

4) Dalet=3 Empress=Binah to Din, #14 Illuminating Intelligence / Illuminating Consciousness

5) Heh=4 Emperor=Keter to Hochmah, #2 Illuminating Intelligence and the splendor of the Unity / Radiant Consciousness

6) Vav=5 Hierophant=Keter to Binah, #5Radical Intelligence / Rooted Consciousness

7) Zayin=6 Lovers=Hochmah to Tifereth, #6 Intelligence of the Mediating Influence / Transcendental Consciousness

8) Chet=7 Chariot=Binah to Tifereth, #9 Pure Intelligence / Pure Consciousness

9) Tet=8 Strength=Chesed to Binah, #11 Scintillating Intelligence / Glaring Consciousness

10) Yod=9 Hermit=Din to Hochmah, #17 Disposing Intelligence / Consciousness of the Senses

11) Kaf =10 Wheel of Fortune=Chesed to Netzach, #18 House of Influence / Consciousness of the House of Influx

12) Lamed=11 Justice= Chesed to Tifereth, #20 Intelligence of Will / Consciousness of the Will

13) Mem=12 Hanged Man= Netzach to Hod, #16 Triumphal or Eternal Intelligence / Enduring Consciousness

14) Nun=13 Death=Din to Tifereth, #22 Faithful Intelligence / Faithful Consciousness

15) Samekh=14 Temperance=Tifereth to Netzach, #27 Exciting Intelligence / Palpable Consciousness

16) Eyin=15 Devil=Tifereth to Hod, #28 Natural Intelligence / Natural Consciousness

17) Peh=16 Tower=Din to Hod, #21 Intelligence of Conciliation / Desired and Sought Consciousness

18) Tzadi=17 Star= Netzach to Yesod, #29 Corporeal Intelligence / Physical Consciousness

19) Kuf=18 Moon=Hod to Yesod, #31 Perpetual Intelligence / Continuous Consciousness

20) Resh=19 Sun=Tifereth to Yesod, #25 Intelligence of Probation /
Testing Consciousness

21) Shin= 20 Judgment= Hochmah to Binah, #24 Imaginative
Intelligence / Apparitive Consciousness

22) Tav=21 World= Yesod to Malkuth, # 32 Administrative
Intelligence / Worshipped Consciousness

One last note, most of the Qabalah books rather than using the ARI
tree use, what I called in my first book *The Gates of Light*, as the Enclosed
Tree. The difference between the ARI tree and the Enclosed Tree is that the
Enclosed Tree does not have the diagonal path from Binah to Chesed nor
the diagonal path from Hochmah to Din. Rather it has a diagonal line from
Hod to Malkuth and from Netzach to Malkuth. I assume that the path of Tet
moves from Hod to Malkuth and the path of Yod moves from Netzach to
Malkuth.

The Sefirahs of the Tree and Magickal Work

Within the Traditional views of Rabbinic Kabbalah, the forces of the sefirahs are in conflict and opposition, and hence the world results in conflict and opposition. There is goodness versus evil, masculine versus feminine, light versus darkness, a dualistic system within the monotheistic Divine.

This disharmony needs to be overcome and repaired. This can be done by the actions of humanity through deeds that restore and heal. Acts of goodness, beauty, truthfulness, and justice can restore and repair this disharmony. That is a major theme of this reclaimed Qabalah.

Potentially each of the sefirahs should not be in disharmony and conflict, but the work of Tikkun Olam is needed and so the Tree is in a state of flux needing attention and repair.

I will give a brief set of the meanings of each of the sefirahs as well as referring to the names from the *Thirty-Two Gates of Wisdom* text as explained on pages 127-135. What will follow will be a brief discussion of the paths. I do not claim to be an expert in the Tarot and the meanings of the major arcana, but I will point and offer suggestions as to the paths' meanings. Others who come after me can more completely flesh out their meanings.

Keter: Crown. This is the Tao, which can be spoken about, which can be partially mapped, yet never can be fully named, and mapped. It points toward Ayn Sof, which is the Tao that cannot be named and cannot be spoken about, and cannot be contained in any map. It is the infinite dynamic interactive nonverbal and non-symbolic totality. It is desire and it is will. #1) Admirable or Concealed Intelligence (Mystical Consciousness)

Hochmah: Wisdom, Supernal Father, Yang, unconscious, symbolic and nonverbal archetypes and ideals, the sum of all possibilities, the seed, potential. The connotations of the Hebrew word are skill and shrewdness, the ability to use and apply information. This is when and where the first presence and manifestation of Divine will and desire comes to and resides. Metaphorically these would be the lower portions of the brain structures. #3) Sanctifying Intelligence (Sanctified Consciousness). My planetary association is Jupiter.

Binah: Understanding, Supernal Mother, Yin, consciousness, verbalization, differentiation, distinction, power of manifestation, birth, formation. The connotations of the Hebrew word discernment, to make distinct, to perceive, and to observe. Metaphorically these would be the two cerebral hemispheres of the brain structures. #7) Occult [as in hidden] Intelligence (Hidden Consciousness). My planetary association is Saturn.

Daat: Knowledge, offspring, and outcome, of wisdom and understanding; completion and resolution. Hebrew root means attachment and union. Daat brings together Hochmah' and Binah. Metaphorically this would be the prefrontal cortex of the brain and the corpus callosum.

Gedulah/Chesed: Gedulah is a feminine term for Greatness. Chesed is a masculine noun for loving-kindness. It as Chesed is associated with Abraham, parental (fatherly) love, obedience, willingness to submit to a greater purpose. In general terms, this sefirah is considered masculine. This is metaphorically the right arm. My Planetary association: Sun. #10) Resplendent Intelligence (Scintillating Consciousness).

Gevurah/Din: Gevurah is a feminine term for Might, power, Din is a masculine noun for governing, making choices and decisions, passing judgments, absolute judgment, and the letter of the law, severity, and limitation. Hebrew word connotations are Also known as Pachad masculine terms for fear. Isaac. In general terms, this sefirah is considered feminine. This is metaphorically the left arm. My Planetary association: Mars. #13) Uniting Intelligence (Unity Directing Consciousness).

Tifereth: This is a feminine noun, Beauty, Glory, and harmony, "The Holy One, Blessed be", the one who balances severe judgment with love to bring about mercy, hence its other name Rachamim-from the root term ReCHeM meaning womb. This is unconditional motherly love and mercy. Tifereth brings the upper Chesed and Din into balance as well as all the lower sefirahs into balance. The lower sefirahs are Chesed, Din, Netzach, Hod, and Yesod. The biblical personality associated with these sefirahs is Jacob, who wrestled with an angel and became Israel. This is the lover and beloved in the Song of Songs and his love and beloved is Malkuth. Through harmony there manifest beauty. This is metaphorically the torso. My Planetary association Neptune. #15) Constituting Intelligence (Stabilizing Consciousness).

It turns out that in my book Qabalah Gates of Light (2014) there is a major error in it. I confused Hod, Netzach, the attribution of Aaron, and Moses, and thus the planets Mercury and the Moon. The correct facts are this:

Netzach = Moses

Hod = Aaron[56]

---

[56] (Drob, Symbols of the Kabbalah: Philosophical and Psychological Perspectives 2000, 196)

This means that Hod is the High Priest, the Occult High Magician, and Mercury. Whereas Netzach is the 'one who is chosen', the receptive, the intuitive, the way of Wicca, the shaman, and thus the Moon.[57]

Netzach: Is a masculine noun, Triumph, eternity, endurance, and timeliness, the endless flowing of events. Netzach channels the powers of the Hochmah and Chesed down to the Earth and humanity. Moses the prophet chosen by the Divine, the mystic, and the shaman, the way of Wicca and earth-based magick. Metaphorically the leg. My Planetary association: Moon. #19) Intelligence of all the activities of the spiritual beings (Consciousness of the mystery of all spiritual activities).

Hod: This is a masculine noun for Majesty, Splendor, timelessness, and vigor when time ceases to move. The time of contemplation and

---

[57] To explain my mistake, it is to recognize the power of unconscious bias. I attributed Aaron the High Priest with the so called 'masculine' attributions of the intellect and the active side. Hence the 'right' pillar with Hochmah must thereby where you place Aaron, hence Aaron 'must be' associated with Netzach. Wrong! Drob told us that according to Moses Cordovero Aaron is not on the 'right' pillar but on the 'so-called' left 'feminine pillar with Binah. Just the opposite of the Western attributions of masculine and feminine. I kept my Western bias and listened to that, when I should have paid attention to the facts that the Rabbis have their own bias concerning masculine and feminine and how they associate it with the Tree. Hence the Rabbis put the active intellect of the High Priest with the 'Feminine Binah/Din (Judgment and discernment) pillar. My Western biased mindset just would not let me clearly see this fact and thus my mistake in my first version of my first book.

meditation. Aaron, the High Priest, the active way of hermetic formal occult magick. Hod channels the powers of Binah and Din down to the Earth and humanity. Metaphorically the leg. My Planetary association: Mercury. #23) Stable Intelligence (Sustaining Consciousness).

Yesod: This is a Hebrew word that is sometimes treated as a masculine noun and other times as a feminine noun. Foundation, creative force and energy, sexual center, and sexual organs both symbolically and metaphorically, traditionally the phallus. My Planetary association: Venus. #26) Renovating Intelligence (Renewing Consciousness).

Malkuth: Kingdom, though a feminine plural word so Queendom. Also known as Shekinah, the indwelling spirit, presence of the Divine. The known God of the Bible. The physical realm. My Planetary association: Earth. #30) Collecting Intelligence (General Consciousness).

The Three Mother Letters and the Horizontal Paths

The Path of Alef, the Fool

Alef = 0 Fool = #8 Absolute or Perfect Intelligence / Perfect Consciousness.

This is the path of the Fool.

Chesed embodies Abraham, and Din embodies Isaac according to Moses Cordovero. Abraham was amazed by the birth of Isaac but was forced to place Isaac under the seeming judgmental eye of the Biblical God when Abraham is instructed to bind Isaac up and sacrifice him on an altar.[58] Abraham's love of God is tested. Isaac's love of his father is tested as well. Both acted with faith and love that all will end up right in the end, but neither knows for certain that it will. Both were subjected to judgment and hoping for mercy and intervention from the Divine. Both were, therefore, judging the Divine, even as the Divine were judging them.

The fool is traveling between parental love and judgment. She seems to be trapped, bouncing between the father's parental love and judgment and/or the parental love and judgment of society.

---

[58] The Book of Genesis Chapter 22

It is a difficult thing to have faith and trust in powers that figuratively or literally hold positions of power of life and death over you, but this is the path of the fool. We have to decide whether to openly and consciously submit and walk the path that parents and society dictate. We can outwardly fight this and travel to a beat of a different drummer. Often if we do this we are judged as being a fool.

We can choose to only seemingly walk the straight and narrow path of expectations while in our hearts and minds we take the inner leap of escape or denial.

Our instincts can be a help or a hindrance on our journey, and things can change over time. The journey changes us and transforms us. We can start the fool and end the wise one. It is the chance we always face. Walking out the door is a dangerous business, the voice of Bilbo Baggins tells us,[59] and we can easily lose our way if we stray from the path.

Unexpected invitations are dancing lessons from the Divine and the fool loves to dance. However, is it the path of expectations, or the path of our intentions, or the path of our inner guide? How can we tell the difference? How can we find our way?

---

[59] (Tolkien 1954-1955, 74) *The Fellowship of the Ring*, Book One, Chapter 3, *Three is Company*.

The Path of Mem, The Hanged Man

Mem=12 Hanged Man= Netzach to Hod, #16 Triumphal or Eternal Intelligence / Enduring Consciousness

This is the path of the Hanged Man. Netzach embodies the High Priest Aaron and Hod embodies the prophet Moses according to Moses Cordovero. How to relate to these two archetypes of the Torah? I see Netzach and Hod are the continua of the connection of humans to the Infinite Divine. At one end of this continuum is the active mode of embodied in Netzach at the other end of this continuum is the receptive mode embodied in Hod. Netzach is the mode of the occult high magician and mystic, while Hod is the mode of the Wiccan and shaman.

The Hanged man is the willingness to give oneself over or deliberately act to enter into altered states. Or it can be the one who suddenly is overwhelmed by an altered state of reality. Such as when you go to sleep and begin to dream. It is to suspend oneself between the worlds, to connect with the beyond, to bridge the upper and lower realms and bring them into human consciousness.

The Hanged man is sacrificed, willingly or not, to some cause or purpose and thereby connecting to that greater force which is Netzach and Hod.

The Hanged man is associated with Odin of the Norse pantheon, he who hung from the world tree, Yggdrasil.

The one who is between light and shadow. Someone who has entered into the 'dark night of the soul'.

Someone who is forced and willing to suspend their disbelief or beliefs.

The Path of Shin, Judgment

Shin= 20 Judgment= Hochmah to Binah, #24 Imaginative Intelligence / Apparitive Consciousness

Shin is on the path between Hochmah and Binah. Hochmah, being, Wisdom, the unconscious mind, the Supernal Father and Binah being Understanding, the conscious mind, the Supernal Mother.

Judgment is the event of being called to awaken to a major or final transformation. Often represented as Judgment day when the dead are called to rise up and be called into account.

To be called to travel between conscious and unconscious forces. To be judged by greater powers, either cosmic, divine, or ones of the mind.

To be engaged in or forced to reevaluate your situation and/or circumstance in light of conscious and unconscious thoughts and/or thought processes.

The Seven Double Letters and the Vertical Paths

As mentioned earlier (pp 102-103), the seven double letters include Resh. The layout of the tree with its seven vertical paths called out for a grouping of seven letters. Was it simply serendipity that the author of the *Sefer Yetzirah* had a copy of the text with those scribal errors? Completely speculating, if the Resh errors had not been noticed the letter Vav could have been called a double letter since it works as both a consonant and as a vowel, it even has two vowel sounds depending on the placement of the dot/dagesh to designate its sound in a pointed text. Therefore, on a purely theoretical basis, the *Sefer Yetzirah* with the path pattern on the Tree both required seven letters to be part of the 'double' letter group, if the Resh was not called into service as a double letter; the Vav might have been used. Of course, this would have changed the letter placement on the Tree, but we do not need to deal with this purely hypothetical issue since the Resh was considered as one of the double letters.

The Path of Bet, The Magician

Beth=1 Magician= Keter to Tifereth, #4 Measuring, Cohesive or Receptacular Intelligence / Settled Consciousness

Bet is the path between Keter and Tifereth going through Daat/Knowledge. Keter is Divine will and Divine desire. Whereas Tifereth is beauty, harmony, the compassion of the womb-of maternal unconditional love.

The Magician is the one who acts with will and desire to bring harmony and compassion for self or others.

The one who taps into desire and will to gain mastery and skill to create beauty and compassion.

The one who consciously recognizes natural beauty and natural harmony to create acts that flow those forces.

The Path of Gimel, The High Priestess

Gimel = 2 High Priestess=Hochmah to Chesed, #12 Intelligence of Transparency / Glowing Consciousness

Gimel is the path between Hochmah and Gedulah/Chesed. The path between Wisdom and Feminine Greatness, Loving Kindness and or parental love. The High Priestess is the one who taps into and flows between the forces and energies of wisdom, greatness, and love. She transmits what she ascertains of the wisdom of love.

She is the one who realizes her inner self or hidden truths because she is connected to greatness, love, and wisdom.

The Path of Dalet, The Empress

Dalet = 3 Empress=Binah to Din, #14 Illuminating Intelligence / Illuminating Consciousness

Dalet is the path between Binah and Gevurah/Din. The path between Understanding and feminine Power and Judgement. Another appellation associated with this sefirah is Pachad meaning masculine fear.

The Empress is the mother goddess, who connects with conscious understanding to wield power and can cause fear. She is the embodiment of what an unenlightened male fears, a woman awakened and consciously understands her power.

The Path of Kaf, The Wheel of Fortune

Kaf =10 Wheel of Fortune=Chesed to Netzach, #18 House of Influence / Consciousness of the House of Influx

Kaf is the path between Gedulah/Chesed and Netzach. The path between feminine Greatness, parental love, and eternity, endurance. Due to this position one faces and endures the ever-changing nature of the greater forces of and consequences of having to adapt to the shifting and changing requirements of paternal love – that is perhaps what creates the spinning wheel of fate and one's fortune.

The Path of Peh, The Lighting Struck Tower

Peh=16 Tower=Din to Hod, #21 Intelligence of Conciliation / Desired and Sought Consciousness

Peh is the path between Gevurah/Din and Hod. The path between feminine Power and Judgement, and Splendor. The results of these forces are the sudden act of awesome splendor that is the forced transformation that is the lightning striking the edifice of the tower, which was your achievements and accomplishments.

The Path of Resh, The Sun

Resh=19 Sun=Tifereth to Yesod, #25 Intelligence of Probation / Testing Consciousness

Resh is the path between Tifereth and Yesod. The path between Beauty, Harmony, Maternal Compassion, and the feminine and masculine source of Foundation[60], the source of the alchemy of sexual transformation and the genitals of the cosmic being that is the Sefiroth.

The sun is our star, the external power that is the source of light, energy, life. It enables us to see and therefore is the foundation of our ability to recognize the beauty of the world around us.

It is the foundation of the energy that brings forth a realization of the beauty in, and of, harmony.

---

[60] The Hebrew word Yesod is treated as either a masculine noun or a feminine noun.

The Path of Tav, The World

Tav=21 World= Yesod to Malkuth, # 32 Administrative Intelligence / Worshipped Consciousness

Tav is the path between Yesod and Malkuth. The path between the feminine and masculine source of Foundation, the source of the alchemy of sexual transformation, and the genitals of the cosmic being that is the Sefiroth and the physical World – our Kingdom or our Queendom.

To travel this path is to bring our sexual being and essence into manifestation to create and procreate a material outcome.

The 12 Elemental Letters and the Diagonal Paths

The Path of Heh, The Emperor

Heh=4 Emperor=Keter to Hochmah, #2 Illuminating Intelligence and the splendor of the Unity / Radiant Consciousness

Heh is the path between Keter and Hochmah. The path between Will/Desire and Unconscious Wisdom. The one who travels this path rules actively. This is the active male principle the one who can rule due to tapping into unconscious wisdom, insights that are formed or come out of our will and desire.

The Path of Vav, The Hierophant

Vav=5 Hierophant=Keter to Binah, #5Radical Intelligence / Rooted Consciousness

Vav is the path between Keter and Binah. The path between Will and Desire, and Understanding, Supernal Mother, Consciousness, she who makes manifest. The Hierophant was the name of the high priest of the Greek Elysian mysteries. To travel this path is to bring into conscious awareness and thus to articulate one's will and desires in order to pass this understanding on to others.

The Path of Zayin, The Lovers

Zayin=6 Lovers=Hochmah to Tifereth, #6 Intelligence of the Mediating Influence / Transcendental Consciousness

Zayin is the path between Hochmah and Tifereth. The path between Wisdom, unconscious awareness, Supernal Father, and Beauty, Harmony and Compassion. This is the recognition of the feminine and the masculine union. The willingness to seek out one's beloved and join together. It is to follow your unconscious towards that someone who inspires you by their beauty to become a harmonious unity.

The Path of Chet, The Chariot

Chet=7 Chariot=Binah to Tifereth, #9 Pure Intelligence / Pure Consciousness

Chet is the path between Binah and Tifereth. The path of Understanding, Supernal Mother, Consciousness and Beauty, Harmony, Compassion. To follow this path is to ride the vehicle, or become the vehicle, of conscious understanding toward beauty and harmony as its outcome.

The Path of Tet, Strength

Tet=8 Strength=Chesed to Binah, #11 Scintillating Intelligence / Glaring Consciousness

Tet is the path between Binah and Gedulah/Chesed going through Daat/Knowledge. The path of Understanding, Supernal Mother, and Consciousness, and feminine Greatness and paternal Loving Kindness. To follow this path is to acknowledge and tap into the power and strength that is the feminine that comes from conscious awareness of feminine greatness and the blessing bestowed by parental love. This will enable you to recognize your inner strength that can work with powerful animal and physical energies.

The Path of Yod, The Hermit

Yod=9 Hermit=Din to Hochmah, #17 Disposing Intelligence / Consciousness of the Senses

Yod is the path between Hochmah and Gevurah/Din, going through Daat/Knowledge. The path of Wisdom, Supernal Father, and the unconscious, and Judgment and feminine Power. To travel this path is to travel it alone, to dwell in unconsciousness by one's self, to not fear the judgment of others and not to be tempted by the call of power but rather to seek wisdom.

The Path of Lamed, Justice

Lamed=11 Justice= Chesed to Tifereth, #20 Intelligence of Will / Consciousness of the Will

Lamed is the path between Chesed/Gedulah and Tifereth. The path between feminine greatness, parental love and beauty, harmony, and unconditional maternal love.

To travel this path is how you find justice; you tame the possible harsh decrees by bringing and uniting harmony with unconditional parental masculine and feminine love and compassion.

The Path of Nun, Death

Nun=13 Death=Din to Tifereth, #22 Faithful Intelligence / Faithful Consciousness

Nun is the path between Gevurah/Din and Tifereth. The path between Beauty, Harmony, and Compassion of unconditional love, and feminine Power and Judgement.

You surrender to the decrees of the judgment of greater powers but hold within the faith of harmony and compassion and thus you plunge and embrace the death of your current existence.

The Path of Samekh, Temperance

Samekh=14 Temperance=Tifereth to Netzach, #27 Exciting Intelligence / Palpable Consciousness

Samekh is the path between Tifereth and Netzach. The path of Beauty, Harmony and Compassion and Eternity, Triumph, timeliness in the never-ending flow of time.

When you travel this path you recognize moderation to temper the effects of time and the physical world as you float between the never-ending flowing river of time and solidity and pull of worldly beauty. By not being pulled into the river currents of by time, you come into triumph over the ordinary realm and dwell in harmony.

The Path of Eyin, The Devil

Eyin=15 Devil=Tifereth to Hod, #28 Natural Intelligence / Natural Consciousness

Eyin is the path between Tifereth and Hod. The path between the glamor of dazzling and alluring beauty, and also with the unconditional acceptance that allows us to be complacent with our flaws and weaknesses and then falling into and getting lost in the timeless moment of now, with the allure of seductive splendor. Getting transfixed in the moment and thus the status quo, being seduced into thinking that nothing can or will change and giving up the possibility of change.

The Devil can be many things but one aspect of this card that I find inspiring came from the Arthurian Deck by Caitlín Matthews and John Matthews. They had the Devil card be 'the Green Knight'. According to that tale, the Green Knight was the trickster challenger who came to King Arthur's Round Table to challenge whoever dared accept this initially unspecified challenge. To deal with the challenge the knight had to realize that it was a riddle to be solved and had to be willing to relinquish one's beliefs in the status quo and to take a leap of faith.

The Devil is the trickster who challenges our accepted norms and beliefs that we are so comfortable with. The Devil comes to shake things up and to get us to realize that we have accepted chains that bind us to the past

and to the status quo. The chains that bind us are not locked; we only need

the self-awareness to awaken to a new perspective to shed them.

The Path of Tzadi, The Star

Tzadi=17 Star= Netzach to Yesod, #29 Corporeal Intelligence / Physical Consciousness

Tzadi is the path between Netzach and Yesod. The path between Triumph, eternity, endurance, timeliness, and Hermetic magick and the foundation, the alchemical, sexual, creative center. The Star is the Feminine who bridges two realms. The focused consciousness and the deep connection to the Cosmos in the unconscious can blend the two in her creative fire of being and transformation. The one who taps into the Cosmic order to create transformation.

The Path of Kuf, The Moon

Kuf=18 Moon=Hod to Yesod, #31 Perpetual Intelligence / Continuous Consciousness

Kuf is the path between Hod and Yesod. The path between Majesty, splendor, timelessness, the mystic, and the shaman, the way of Wicca and earth-based magick, and the foundation, the alchemical center of sexual creative transformation. Getting lost in or following, the cycle of change and transformation. The way of the mystic, the shaman, and the witch is this path allowing oneself to dwell into the splendor of timelessness that is gestation and transformation, and getting lost in the moment and the illusion that it lasts forever.

The Two Paths that create the Enclosed Tree

To create the Enclosed Tree the tree so often used in books about the Occult Qabalah you have to imagine taking the ARI Tree (see Figure 7) and removing the Tet path connecting Binah and Chesed and placing it so that it becomes a path connecting Hod and Malkuth. Additionally, you remove the Yod path connecting Hochmah and Din and placing it so that it becomes a path connecting Netzach and Malkuth.

Hod to Malkuth: The Path of Tet

Tet=8 Strength, #11 Scintillating Intelligence / Glaring Consciousness

This is the path between Majesty, splendor, timelessness, the mystic, and the shaman, the way of Wicca and earth-based magick and Kingdom/Queendom, the Shekinah, the indwelling spirit, presence of the Divine., the physical realm. To follow this path is to connect to the earth and the physical to draw strength for inner and outer work. To tame the physical beast and draw upon it. To call upon its splendor and timeless strength.

Netzach to Malkuth: The Path of Yod

Yod=9 Hermit, #17 Disposing Intelligence / Consciousness of the Senses

The path between triumph, eternity, endurance, timeliness, the active way of hermetic formal occult magick and Kingdom/Queendom, the Shekinah, the indwelling spirit, presence of the Divine., the physical realm. The solitary travel that dwells within while traveling in the physical realm. The one who actively pursues knowledge to gain access to eternal wisdom through the connection to our indwelling divine spirit and the physical world around us.

The Major Arcana and the GRA 1884 Tree

What would the Major Arcana placement on the GRA 1884 Tree as shown in figure 8 look like? What if you wanted to work with the GRA's Tree, what I am calling the hypothetical plan before the events of creation that then shattered the spheres and rendered the existing Tree as depicted in the Zohar/ARI array.

Here are the paths and the cards referencing the GRA's Tree pattern of figure 8.

Path of the Fool: Chesed to Gevurah/Din

Path of the Magician: Keter to Daat

Path of the High Priestess: Hochmah to Gedulah/Chesed

Path of the Empress: Binah to Gevurah/Din

Path of the Emperor: Keter to Hochmah

Path of the Hierophant: Keter to Binah

Path of the Lovers: Hochmah to Daat

Path of the Chariot: Binah to Daat

Path of Strength: Daat to Gedulah/Chesed

Path of the Hermit: Daat to Gevurah/Din

Path of the Wheel of Fortune: Gedulah/Chesed to Netzach

Path of Justice: Gedulah/Chesed to Tifereth

Path of the Hanged Man: Netzach to Hod

Path of Death: Gevurah/Din to Tifereth

Path of Temperance: Tifereth to Netzach

Path of the Devil: Tifereth to Hod

Path of the Tower: Gevurah/Din to Hod

Path of the Star: Netzach to Yesod

Path of the Moon: Hod to Yesod

Path of the Sun: Tifereth to Yesod

Path of Judgment: Hochmah to Binah

Path of the World: Yesod to Malkuth

Conclusion: Find Your Way

My work here is done. I've completed as much as I wanted to at this point in time. I have reclaimed the Qabalah from false Christian influences and returned it to the metaphors and symbols of the Rabbis.

Whereas in the old Christian inspired Qabalah the Tree existed as this dead and abstract glyph that had no inherent meaning and needed outside symbols and metaphors to hung on the tree like Christmas ornaments and to be used and then discarded when you were done using it like some dead and dried up Christmas tree with the needles falling off it and the ornaments were taken off it.

Now, instead, you have a living tree, the Cosmic Tree of Life and Knowledge with its roots in Gan Eden and reaching deep into the earth and reaching up and touching the starry heavens above. It always is there alive and waiting for you to come to it and study its mysteries, its wisdom, and its meanings.

I have explained how you are a part of this living entity; it is a part of all things in the cosmos. The Kabbalistic Rabbis taught that all your actions have consequences, cosmic consequences. You are here if you so choose to listen to the song of Tikkun Olam and are willing to participate in restoring, repairing, and healing yourself, the cosmos, and the Divine

Herself. As below, so above!

Every act of goodness, truth, beauty, and justice brings harmony to

the spheres, the cosmos, and the Divine. They are all acts of Tikkun Olam.

Working with the Tree is all a part of this great plan and hope of the

Divine, known as Ayn Sof and Shekinah.

As Rabbi Tarfon (circa 70 CE – 135) is recorded as saying in the *Pirke*

Avot (The Sayings of the Fathers) '*It is not your duty to finish the work, but you*

are not a liberty to neglect it. [61]'You need to find your way of coming to terms

with the reclaimed Qabalah and make it part of your own magickal and

spiritual practice. There are many Qabalah books that now are in need of

reworking and rewriting, perhaps you will be the one to write one of them.

---

[61] (Goldin 1955, 116)

Appendix 1: After The Garden My Aggadah.[62]

What happened to the characters of the story after they left the Garden? In the text:

Genesis 5:4 And the days of Adam after he begot Seth were eight hundred years, and he begot sons and daughters.

5: 5 And all the days that Adam lived were nine hundred and thirty years, and he died. [63] However, I am looking for more insights into the life that Eve, Adam, Lilith all made for themselves.

Therefore, as the story continues…Eve and Adam set out from Gan Eden to build a life together and with their children. The world becomes inhabited and a home for humanity that gathered in villages. Now, Lilith, after merging with the Tree and eating its fruits left the Garden to go forth and explored the planet, studying the plants and animals, learning their abilities and their properties. She discovered the secrets of the plants and how they could be used. Then she set off to explore the heavens above.

---

[62] The idea to create this tale came to me during a meditation led by Alix Wright, witch, teacher and High Priestess with the Temple of Witchcraft Mystery School, who was leading a ritual of empowerment invoking Lilith. This ritual took place on Monday February 19, 2018, at the 24th PantheaCon held at the Double Tree Hotel in San Jose, California.

[63] (Jewish Publication Society 1917)

Eventually, she returned to Earth and found that the lands surrounding Gan Eden were inhabited by the descendants of Adam and Eve. Lilith saw that some were getting ill and they did not know the healing arts and did not know how to return to the Garden and merge and make use of the powers of the Tree. She felt sorry for them and decided to help. She became the wise woman of the woods and of the mountains, a witch, and a healer.

Many would seek her out for her help and healing. However, some would fear her and drive her off. In this way, she would wander the lands, mainly alone and aloof.

She would generally live in the outskirts, in the wild zones beyond towns, villages, and cities; in forests or caves.

As time went on, she would notice that some ravens and crows seemed to be following her movements.

One day, while she was in the forest seeking herbs for her study and practice she noticed the calling of the crows. As she looked up from her work she saw approaching a young girl, who called out to Lilith.

"Are you my Auntie Lilith?" The girl asked.

Lilith was surprised and amused. "I am known as Lilith, but I am not sure I am anyone's Aunt? Who are you and what are you doing so far from your home?"

"I am Ilana. I was told that our crow, Night Watch, would lead me to my Auntie."

"The crow is your pet?"

"Yes, my Daddy trained it. I was told to follow her and then to bring you back to our home in the village."

"You were, were you? Who instructed you with this task?"

"My Mommy, she is Eve."

"Really? And is your Daddy named Adam?"

"Yes. Do you have anything sweet to eat? I would like that, and something cool to drink and then could you go with me back to our home? Night Watch, the crow will lead us."

"Well, I guess I will. Come, let's find you something to eat and drink, and then we will go meet your Mommy and Daddy."

And so Lilith was led back to Eve and Adam by the crow and the young girl, her niece Ilana. There she learned that Eve and Adam had been searching for Lilith for many years. They wished that she would teach their daughters and some of their sons in the ways of the Tree of Life and

Knowledge since Lilith knew more of those mysteries than either Eve or

Adam. And so it was that Lilith came to dwell with Eve and Adam and teach

the children. And in this way, wisdom and mystery was passed down the

ages.

Appendix 2: Ritual Frame

I offer the following possible ritual frame for your magickal workings with the Tree of Life and Knowledge.

***

[You stand facing the East.]

I come to the border between this world and the other.

I come to the land that our cosmic ancestors left to renew our connection to the source.

I come stripping away shame[64]

I come stripping away fear

I come stripping away guilt

I come stripping away innocence

I come with pride

I come with courage

I come with justice

I come with experience

And thus the flaming sword does not bar my way.

I enter Gan Eden

---

[64] Question to the reader: Do these four terms, shame, fear, guilt and innocence with their opposites represent a sefirah?

I return to the source.

I stand facing the rising sun

KETER (touch brow with two fingers)

MALKUTH (point to your feet)

YESOD (touch groin)

VE-GEBURAH (touch right shoulder)

VE-GEDULAH (touch left shoulder)

LE-OLAM (arms crossed across the breast)

AMEN (palms together)

(Conjuring pentagrams at each direction.)

(Turn to the East:) YOD-HE-VAV-HE! HA SHEM!

(Turn to the South): ADONAI! O' LORD!

(Turn to the West): EHEIEH (eh-ee-eh!) I AM THAT I AM!

(Turn to the North): ATAH GIVOR LE'OLAM ADONAI! YOU, O LORD, ARE MIGHT FOREVER!

(Return to facing East)

Hail Auriael before me, guardian of the East, keeper of the sword of discernment. [Conjure a sword]

Hail Raphael behind me, guardian of the West, keeper of the cup of feelings [conjure a cup]

Hail Mikhael to my right, guardian of the South, keeper of the flaming staff of energy [conjure a staff]

Hail Gav'riael to my left, guardian of the North, Keeper of the pentacle of the physical [conjure a pentacle]

By all that is below [conjure the earth in space]

By all that is above [conjure the moon, the sun, and finally the stars]

I stand at the base of the Tree of Life and Knowledge [conjure the Tree of Life]

I have come here to stand in the center of all the worlds.

I stand in the center to take on the role of the Tree of Life and Knowledge.

I am the tree that is the bridge between the sacred spaces of Above, Below, and Between.

I am the bridge that unites the realms of Atziluth / Emanation (Visualize Hochmah that is the right side of your face as glowing);

Beriah/Creation (Visualize Binah as the left side of your face as glowing);

Yetzirah/ Formation (visualize Chesed as your right side of your chest, shoulder, and arm, Din as your left side of your chest, shoulder, and arm, Tifereth as your stomach, Netzach as your right hip and leg, Hod as your left hip and leg, and Yesod as your genitals, all of these areas are glowing.);

And Assiah / Action. (Visualize your feet and the earth beneath them as glowing.)

What is done here can heal and change all the worlds.

[Set out candles, can be one, two, or three. If one it should be white, if two one is white the other black, if there, white, black, and the center candle is a colored candle. The candles represent the one offering, or the twin pillars or the three pillars of the Tree.]

B'ruchah Shekinah, malcah ha-Olam, boray m'oray ha-aysh.

Let us bless Shekinah, Queen of the cosmos, creator of the light of fire.

{Light the Candle(s).]

[Continue with your main working at this point in the ritual.]

I recognize that I was the bridge that unites the realms of Assiah / Action. (Visualize your feet and the earth beneath them as glowing.);

Yetzirah/ Formation (visualize Yesod as your genitals, Hod as your left hip and leg, Netzach as your right hip and leg, Tifereth as your stomach, Din as your left side of your chest, shoulder, and arm, and Chesed as your right side of your chest, shoulder, and arm, all of these areas are glowing.);

Beriah/Creation (Visualize Binah as the left side of your face as glowing);

And Atziluth, Emanations (Visualize Hochmah which is the right side of your face as glowing.

I was the tree that was the bridge between the sacred spaces of Above, Below, and Between.

I stood in the center and took on the role of the Tree of Life and Knowledge.

I now relinquish conscious awareness of being the Tree I become conscious of my own body that stood before the Tree at the center of Gan Eden.

By all that was above, I thank thee ere I depart. [look upwards and pull in the energies of the stars, the sun, and the moon and bring them to your head and heart.]

By all that was below, I thank thee ere I depart. [Look down and pull the energy of the earth and bring it to your head and heart.]

[Face North and see the pentacle that you had conjured.] Hail Gav'riael guardian of the North, Keeper of the pentacle of the physical. I thank thee ere I depart. [Bring the pentacle into your head and heart.]

[Face West and see the cup that you had conjured.] Hail Raphael guardian of the West, keeper of the cup of feelings. I thank thee ere I depart. [Bring the cup into your head and heart.]

[Face South and see the staff that you had conjured.] Hail Mikhael guardian of the South, keeper of the flaming staff of energy. I thank thee ere I depart. [Bring the staff into your head and heart.]

[Face the East and see the sword that you had conjured.] Hail Auriael guardian of the East, keeper of the sword of discernment. I thank you ere I depart. [Bring the sword into your head and heart.]

I leave Gan Eden with Experience, with Justice, with courage, and with pride.

I pass beyond the flaming sword that protects Gan Eden as I depart to the realm of the ordinary.

Baruchah at Shekinah, malcah ha-olam, hamavdeel bayn kodesh l'chol, bayn or l'choshech. Baruchah at Shekinah, hamavdeel bayn Kodesh l'chol.

Blessed is the Shekinah, Queen of the cosmos, who separates the sacred from the ordinary, light from the darkness. Blessed is the Shekinah, Queen of the cosmos, who separates the sacred from the ordinary.

The circle is open but unbroken.

We stand again on ordinary ground. Let holy lights illumine our hearts. And our memory holds all, 'ere we depart.

Blessed Be.

Appendix 3: Tarot Spreads as Major Workings in A Ritual

Here are some tarot spreads that can be used in your work.

#1 Shekinah's Challenge

This is one I have been doing every dark moon since March of 2017. I would ask Shekinah what challenge She has for me in between this dark moon and the next.

First card: The physical challenge

Second card: An intellectual insight and understanding of that challenge.

Third card: An emotional insight and understanding of that challenge.

#2 Days of Future Passed Spread

Three cards would mark out the events of the present, and then three cards would offer a look at potential events of the future.

First card: the current situation

Second card: Intellectual insight and understanding of the present

Third card: Emotional insight and understanding of the present

Fourth card: Potential future situation

Fifth card: Intellectual insight and understanding of that future

Sixth card: Emotional insight and understanding of that future.

#3 Climbing the Tree spread

First card: Malkuth

Second card: Netzach and the channeled energies from Chesed

Third card: Hod and the channeled energies from Din

Fourth card: Daat (your manifested desire and will)

Fifth card: Hochmah (understanding of Daat card)

Sixth card: Binah (wisdom of Daat card)

#4 & 5: The Two 32 Gates of Wisdom spreads are an excellent way to get used to working with and understanding the meaning of the paths on the Tree.

#4 The 32 Gates of Wisdom utilizing the Zohar/ARI Tree

Doing this spread might be a once-a-year event. Gather all the major arcana cards in one pile. Then separate all of the minor arcana cards by putting all the court cards together, all the Aces together, all the twos, all the threes, etc.

First card: shuffle the Aces and pick one. Place it at the Keter point on the Tree.

Second card: shuffle the twos and pick one. Place it at the Hochmah point on the Tree.

Third card: shuffle the threes and pick one. Place it at the Binah point on the Tree.

Fourth card: shuffle all the court cards and pick one. Place it at the Daat point on the Tree.

Fifth card: shuffle all the fours and pick one. Place it at the Chesed point on the Tree.

Sixth card: shuffle all the fives and pick one. Place it at the Din point on the Tree.

Seventh card: shuffle all the sixes and pick one. Place it at the Tifereth point on the Tree.

Eighth card: shuffle all the sevens and pick one. Place it at the Netzach place on the Tree.

Ninth card: shuffle all the eights and pick one. Place it at the Hod place on the Tree.

Tenth card: shuffle all the nines and pick one. Place it at the Yesod place on the Tree.

Eleventh card: shuffle all the tens and pick one. Place it at the Malkuth place on the Tree.

Now take all the Major Arcana cards and place them on the tree at the fixed assignments as shown on page 179.

Study the Tree and how the paths affect and describe the cards you have chosen at the sefirahs points.

5 The 32 Gates of Light Utilizing the GRA's Tree

Doing this spread might be a once-a-year event. Gather all the major arcana cards in one pile. Then separate all of the minor arcana cards by putting all the court cards together, all the Aces together, all the twos, all the threes, etc.

First card: shuffle the Aces and pick one. Place it at the Keter point on the Tree.

Second card: shuffle the twos and pick one. Place it at the Hochmah point on the Tree.

Third card: shuffle the threes and pick one. Place it at the Binah point on the Tree.

Fourth card: shuffle all the fours and pick one. Place it at the Daat point on the Tree.

Fifth card: shuffle all the fives and pick one. Place it at the Chesed point on the Tree.

Sixth card: shuffle all the sixes and pick one. Place it at the Din point on the Tree.

Seventh card: shuffle all the sevens and pick one. Place it at the Tifereth point on the Tree.

Eighth card: shuffle all the eights and pick one. Place it at the Netzach place on the Tree.

Ninth card: shuffle all the nines and pick one. Place it at the Hod place on the Tree.

Tenth card: shuffle all the tens and pick one. Place it at the Yesod place on the Tree.

Eleventh card: shuffle all the court cards and pick one. Place it at the Malkuth place on the Tree.

Now take all the Major Arcana cards and place them on the tree at the fixed assignments as shown on page 173.

Study the Tree and how the paths affect and describe the cards you have chosen at the sefirahs points.

Appendix 4: Cosmic Evil in Rabbinic Literature[65].

Another source of evil is found on the left side of the Sefiroth, the side where Din is located is considered "The Other Side" the 'Sitra Achara'. When Din is cut off from Chesed, Loving Kindness, or is not balanced by Tifereth/Rachamim, Beauty and Mercy, it acts with pure unadulterated Justice and this again is a source of evil, by beginning judgment without any mercy.

Lastly, the third concept of cosmic evil is the idea that HaSatan, the being mentioned in the book of Job and the character Lilith, are beings of evil. Satan in Aggadahic/Midrashic literature is the leader of the oppositional forces. He is the Evil general opposed to the forces of Good lead by God. Although the Rabbis never go the extremes of Manicheism and Persian mythology were two opposite and equal beings and forces, which fight it out for the hearts, minds, and souls of humanity. Satan in the Job text is a title and not a proper name of the being. In later material, Satan is given the name of Samael. The Hebrew means 'the venom or poison or blindness

---

[65] For an exploration of the Biblical idea of Evil, read Jon D. Levenson's book *Creation and the Persistence of Evil*.

of God'. Besides being the Accuser, HaSatan, as in Job, he is also the angel of death and destruction.

In some of the material, Eve is made a villainess or at least an accomplice by being seduced and mated with to become the mother of demons.

Whereas other Aggadahic /Midrashic material utilizes or recognizes the existence of another Biblical character and lets her be the consort or queen of evil. This is Lilith. The idea of Lilith stems from a reference in Isaiah 34:14.

> *'And the wild-cats shall meet with the jackals, And the satyr shall cry to his fellow; Yea, the LYLYT shall repose there, And shall find her a place of rest.'*[66]
> *The Hebrew word Lamed-Yod-Lamed-Yod-Tav that appears in the Masoretic text. Now theoretically the word should have been LYLH for the singular word for night. Then the text would have been translated as something like ' And the wild cats shall meet with the jackals, and the satyr shall cry to his fellow, the darkness of the night shall be there and they shall find their place of rest.'*

By 'misspelling' that word into first a plural LYLT and then the scribal error of adding an additional Yod turned the word into the feminine form of plural 'Night' a personification of the night; a being of darkness, the

---

66 (Jewish Publication Society 1917)

Lilith. As a result of that scribal error in the Masoretic text a new being was

born, which gave rise to the following Talmudic references:

> *There are three references to Lilith in the Babylonian Talmud in*
> *Gemara on three separate Tractates of the Mishnah:*
> *"Rab Judah citing Samuel ruled: If an abortion had the likeness of*
> *Lilith its mother is unclean by reason of the birth, for it is a child*
> *but it has wings." (Babylonian Talmud on Tractate Nidda*
> *24b)[42]*
> *"[Expounding upon the curses of womanhood] In a Baraitha it*
> *was taught: She grows long hair like Lilith, sits when making*
> *water like a beast, and serves as a bolster for her husband."*
> *(Babylonian Talmud on Tractate Eruvin 100b)*
> *"R. Hanina said: One may not sleep in a house alone [in a lonely*
> *house], and whoever sleeps in a house alone is seized by Lilith."*
> *(Babylonian Talmud on Tractate Shabbath 151b)*
> *The above statement by Hanina may be related to the belief that*
> *nocturnal emissions engendered the birth of demons:*
> *"R. Jeremiah b. Eleazar further stated: In all those years [130*
> *years after his expulsion from the Garden of Eden] during which*
> *Adam was under the ban he begot ghosts and male demons and*
> *female demons [or night demons], for it is said in Scripture: And*
> *Adam lived a hundred and thirty years and begot a son in own*
> *likeness, after his own image, from which it follows that until that*
> *time he did not beget after his own image… When he saw that*
> *through him death was ordained as punishment he spent a*
> *hundred and thirty years in fasting, severed connection with his*
> *wife for a hundred and thirty years, and wore clothes of fig on his*
> *body for a hundred and thirty years. – That statement [of R.*
> *Jeremiah] was made in reference to the semen which he emitted*
> *accidentally." (Babylonian Talmud on Tractate Eruvin 18b)*
> *According to Rabbi Hiyya God proceeded to create a second Eve*
> *for Adamactually after Lilith had to return to dust (Genesis*
> *Rabbah 22:7 and 18:4)*[67]

---

[67] Wikipedia, https://en.wikipedia.org/wiki/Lilith#Hebrew_text.

Lilith and HaSatan according to further Midrashim, became

consorts and out of their coupling, they begat demons.

> *After God created Adam, who was alone, He said, 'It is not good for man to be alone.' He then created a woman for Adam, from the earth, as He had created Adam himself, and called her Lilith. Adam and Lilith immediately began to fight. She said, 'I will not lie below,' and he said, 'I will not lie beneath you, but only on top. For you are fit only to be in the bottom position, while I am to be the superior one.' Lilith responded, 'We are equal to each other inasmuch as we were both created from the earth.' But they would not listen to one another. When Lilith saw this, she pronounced the Ineffable Name and flew away into the air.*
> *Adam stood in prayer before his Creator: 'Sovereign of the universe!' he said, 'the woman you gave me has run away.' At once, the Holy One, blessed be He, sent these three angels Senoy, Sansenoy, and Semangelof, to bring her back.*
> *Said the Holy One to Adam, 'If she agrees to come back, what is made is good. If not, she must permit one hundred of her children to die every day.' The angels left God and pursued Lilith, whom they overtook in the midst of the sea, in the mighty waters wherein the Egyptians were destined to drown. They told her God's word, but she did not wish to return. The angels said, 'We shall drown you in the sea.'*
> *'Leave me!' she said. 'I was created only to cause sickness to infants. If the infant is male, I have dominion over him for eight days after his birth, and if female, for twenty days.'*
> *When the angels heard Lilith's words, they insisted she go back. But she swore to them by the name of the living and eternal God: 'Whenever I see you or your names or your forms in an amulet, I will have no power over that infant.' She also agreed to have one hundred of her children die every day. Accordingly, every day one hundred demons perish, and for the same reason, we write the angels' names on the amulets of young children. When Lilith sees their names, she remembers her oath, and the child recovers.[68]*
> *[Source: Alphabet of Ben Sira]*

---

[68] Wikipedia, https://en.wikipedia.org/wiki/Lilith#Hebrew_text.

Lilith becomes another personification of cosmic evil; she is the female version to complement the male version of Samael, the Satan.

Appendix 5: The Metaphoric Meaning of Yang & Yin

Throughout the understanding of the Sefiroth, the Tree, symbolism runs the metaphors of masculine and feminine. Hochmah and Chesed are considered masculine and hence this pillar is therefore considered the masculine/Yang pillar, whereas Binah and Din are considered feminine and hence this is considered the feminine/Yin pillar.

Now, which is the left and which is the right?

> *The division of the Sefirot into three lines or columns was especially important: the right hand column includes Hokhmah, Gedullah, and Netzach; the left hand column includes Binah, Gevurah, and Hod; and the central column (kav emza'i) passes from Keter through Tiferet and Yesod to Malkut.*[69]

Now for some Kabbalists, they associated one binary system with another binary system, like the fallacy of the Greeks such as Plato and Aristotle, making the mistake of treating all dualities with the overlay of the duality of moral judgments of Good vs Bad. One side of any duality then becomes 'good' while the opposite side of the duality is considered 'bad'. For example:

> *...we already find in the Sefer ha-Bahir a definition of the Sefirah Gevurah, as "the left hand of the Holy One blessed be He," and as*

---

[69] (Scholem, Kabbalah 1974, 109)

"a quality whose name is evil" and which has many offshoots in the forces of judgment, the constricting and limiting powers in the universe.[70] [71]

So, we have a set of Rabbis saying that the left side is where Binah, Din and Hod are. Binah is traditionally thought of as the primal Mother, hence the left side in this system of attributes is Yin/feminine as well as being the side that has a 'source of evil', all not exactly an unbiased appraisal of things. How can we avoid such bias and such sexist attributions?

For one thing, we need to stop Aristotelian logic with its oppositional duality from taking over our thinking of conceptual abstract stuff. Aristotelian logic is good for the analysis of concrete physical stuff but it doesn't work as well when we want to understand abstract non-physical stuff such as concepts. We need non-Aristotelian logic that allows for the middle ground and context-sensitive multiple identifying meanings to a concept. We thus do not automatically associate all dualities with the oppositional morality of the only choice being good or bad/evil. Duality is

---

[70] (Scholem, Kabbalah 1974, 123)

[71] Now this attributing 'evil' with the sefirah of Din is picked up by Isaac the blind, then by the Gerona Kabbalists and the Zohar (Scholem, Kabbalah 1974, 123) and becomes the idea that Din not balanced by Tifereth bringing in the forces of Hesed, creates this strict judgment and thus 'evil' or the 'Other Side'.

not in opposition but merely possible endpoints on a continuum of choices and good and bad are not meaningful, and should not be blindly associated with any of the possible ends points.

So therefore left and right, Yin/female and Yang/male are not in any way related to the continuum of good and bad.

As for Yin and Yang, what if some of those attributes were switched? What is the metaphoric meaning of Yin/Feminine and Yang/Masculine?

Here is what I assume would be a listing of Yin/Yang terms and meanings.

Yang: Solar, Mars, day, intellectual, mind, immaterial, consciousness, active, explicit, analytic, linear, The Creative & Heaven (I Ching), light, verbal, causality, seed.

Yin: Lunar, Venus, night, sensual, passionate, body, material, unconscious, receptive or passive, implicit, holistic, intuitive, nonlinear, The Receptive & Earth (I Ching), dark, non-verbal, emotions, acausal, womb.

Yet, why is Chesed meaning loving-kindness and thus the emotions considered masculine for the Rabbis? While Din meaning strict judgment and discernment is considered feminine for the Rabbis? I think the answer lies in Freudian psychology. The Rabbis and the Hebrews invented patriarchy and all that it implies. They helped to create the sexist stereotypes of good being associated with the masculine and bad with the feminine. Therein lays the clue. For them good was the emotion of loving-kindness and bad was strict judgment. The feminine side with Din was connected to evil, 'the Other Side', the forces of Darkness led by Satan and Lilith.

Yet the Rabbis I think would agree with that list of Yin and Yang attributes. Hence, we are left with a puzzle in treating Chesed and therefore Netzach as Yang/Masculine and Din and Hod as Yin/Feminine.

Perhaps I can make a radical suggestion and change some of the meanings of sefirahs and their associations with Yin & Yang.

My radical suggestion is to allow in a context that the whole right pillar would be Yin/Feminine and make the whole left pillar Yang/Masculine. This would result in Hochmah (unconscious and becomes Supernal Mother), Chesed (feelings/emotions), and Netzach being Yin. That would mean that Binah (conscious and becomes Supernal Father), Din (judgment & discernment), and Hod being Yang.

A radical break with the Rabbinic traditional meanings.

But, does it make sense?

Perhaps the answer lies in alternating the designations of Yin and Yang. Perhaps we just have to adapt to what we are given. Thus Hochmah is the seed and the unconscious, but still Yang. Whereas Binah is the Womb

but also consciousness and Yin. What about Din and Chesed? They seem to

be judgment and analysis contrasted with loving-kindness, feelings,

emotions, and intuition? Yet, which is Yin and which is Yang? Does it really

matter?

What about Netzach and Hod? I considered Hod as the masculine,

Yang, and the conscious, ceremonial magician. I considered Netzach as the

feminine, Yin, unconscious, intuitive, shaman, and Wiccan. Does that still

work?

Perhaps I just need to remove the concept that the attributes of the

right pillar are Yang Masculine and the left pillar is Yin Feminine?

Perhaps what is being taught to us is the true meaning of the

sefirahs is that they are all bisexual.

> That the Kabbalists…viewed the entire cosmos in erotic terms is
> evident from their conceptualization of the dynamic relationships
> among the Sefiroth as a series of Yichudim, or sexual unions
> between the various personas within the godhead. For Luria the
> Breaking of the Vessels, for example, is conceptualized as a
> disruption in these erotic unions, and Tikkun Olam as their
> resumption. The Kabbalists views can also be gleamed from what
> they say about the mental states that must accompany the
> performance of the commandments and prayer. For Luria, such
> states are achieved through the recitation and meditation upon
> various kavvanot (intentions) and Yichudim (unions) whereby
> the adherent concentrates upon performing a particular mitzvah
> for the purpose of unifying divergent aspects of the deity and

thereby healing the fault within both the world and humanity. Typical among these mediations is a prayer that seeks to unite God and Shekinah, the masculine and feminine principles of the universe. Frequently the feminine principle or bride is thought of as the people Israel.

These Kavvanot and Yichudim frequently utilize the symbolism of sexual intercourse. The unification of the Sefiroth is spoken of as a zivvug, coupling between the Celestial Father and Mother or between ...Tiferet and the female principle, Malkuth or Shekhinah. In order for the appropriate unification to take place, mutual male and female orgasms are necessary. The Yichudim help to reunify a deity who embodies both male and female cosmic principles. Such bisexuality is for the Kabbalists an expression of the supreme perfection, a theme that is particularly salient in the Zohar, where we learn that it is incumbent not only for God but also for humanity to become 'male and female' (Zohar I, 49b, Vol. I, 158, Harry Sperling and Maurice Simon, The Zohar, Soncino Press, 1931-1934.).[72]

The Kabbalists made prolific use of sexual and erotic imagery designed to express the notion that the Sefiroth are dynamic, living forces through which divine procreative energy flows into the lower worlds. The Sefirah Yesod is spoken of as the male genitalia, and the final Sefirah, Malkuth, is the image of the female (the Shekinahh), which is the necessary complement and completion of the Primordial Being. Both humanity and the cosmos in general can only be considered whole where there is a direct and harmonious coupling of male and female. Without woman, the Zohar tells us, man is defective, a mere "half body" (Zohar, II 23a – 23b, Vol. I 298, Isaiah Tishby and Fischel Lachower, The Wisdom of the 'Zohar: An Anthology of Texts, The Littman Library of Jewish Civilization, 1994).

Each Sefirah is understood to be male to the Sefirah below it, and female to the Sefirah above it, and the entire cosmic scheme is said to depend upon the proper channeling of the Sefiroth's erotic energy[73]

---

[72] Sanford L. Drob, Kabbalistic Metaphors: Jewish Mystical Themes in Ancient and Modern Thought, Jason Aronson, Inc. 2000, 170-171

[73] Drob, ibid, 51.

Therefore, to assign Yin/Feminine and Yang/Masculine to any pillar or any single sefirah is a mistaken and/or incomplete understanding. Hence. In the end, I would just leave everything as it is but expand my own understanding.

Perhaps the two sides are not either left or right, male or female but both. Imagine that the whole Tree rotates along the middle pillar and in one context the side with Binah/Din/Hod is considered the left side and in another context, the same side is considered the right side. This would also go a long way to decide how the Tree fits on our bodies.

Appendix 6: The Pillars: Middle, Right And Left

The three pillars of the Tree consist of the following sefirahs:

Middle Pillar: Keter, (Daat), Tifereth, Yesod, and Malkuth

The Right Pillar: Hochmah, Gedulah/Chesed, and Netzach

The Left Pillar: Binah, Gevurah/Din, and Hod

Bibliography

Blau, Joseph Leon. *The Christian Interpretation of the Cabala in the Renaissance.*
Kessinger Reprint. New York: Columbia University Press, 1944.

Blumenthal, David R. *understanding Jewish Mysticism: A Source Reader The Merkabah Tradition and the Zoharic Tradition.* New York: KTAV Publishing House Inc., 1978.

Case, Paul Foster. *The Tarot, a Key to Wisdom of the Ages.* First Revised Edition 1990. Los Angeles: Builders of the Adytum, 1947.

Chen, Ellen M. *In Praise of Nothing: An Exploration of Daosit Fundamental Ontology.* Xlibris Corporation, 2011.

—. *The Tao Te Ching: A New Translation with Commentary.* St. Paul: Paragon House, A New Era Book, 1989.

Cicero, Chic, and Sandra Tabatha Cicero. *A Garden of Pomegranates: Skrying on the Tree of Life.* St. Paul: Llewellyn, 1999.

Crowley, Aleister. *Liber 777 And Other Qabalistic Writings of Aleister Crowley Including Gematria & Sepher Sephiroth.* First Paperback edition 1986. Edited by Israel Regardie. York Beach: Samuel Weiser, Inc., 1907, 1909, 1947, 1973.

—. "The Book of Thoth from Equinox Volume 3 no. 5." *Ra-Hoor-Khuit Network.*   March   1,   1998.

www.rahoorkhuit.net/library/crowley/volume3/vol_3_no_05.pdf
(accessed February 3, 2013).

—. "The New and Old Commentaries to Liber Al vel Legis, The Book of the
Law by Aleister Crowley." *The Hermetic Library.* 1996.
hermetic.com/legis/new-comment/ (accessed November 24, 2012).

—. "The New-Comment." *The New and Old Commentaries to Liber Al vel Legis,
The Book of the Law by Aleister Crowley.* 1996.
hermetic.com/legis/new-comment/ (accessed November 24, 2012).

Drob, Sanford L. *Kabbalistic Metaphors: Jewish Mystical Themes in Ancient and
Modern Thought.* Northvale: Jason Aronson, Inc., 2000.

—. *Symbols of the Kabbalah: Philosophical and Psychological Perspectives.*
Northvale: Jason Aronson, Inc., 2000.

Duquette, Lon Milo. *The Chicken Qabalah of Rabbi Lamed Ben Clifford: A
Dilettante's Guide to What You Do and Do Not Need to Know to Become
a Qabalist.* York Beach: Weiser Books, 2001.

Fortune, Dion. *The Mystical Qabalah.* Second American Paperback edition
1999. York Beach: Samuel Weiser, Inc., 1935.

Gikatilla, Rabbi Joseph. *Sha'are Orah: The Gates of Light.* First English
Translation. Translated by Avi Weinstein. San Francisco:
HarperCollins Publishers, 1994.

Gilbert, R. A. *William Wynn Westcott and the Esoteric School of Masonic Research*. Grand Lodge of British Columbia and Yukon, 1987.

Goldin, Judah. *The Living Talmud: The Wisdom of the Fathers (and its Classical Commentaries selected and translated.)*. 7th printing 1957. New York: Mentor Book from New American Library, 1955.

Gurney, J. "Tarot of the Golden Dawn." *Journal of the Western Mystery Tradition*. Autumnal Equinox 2009. http://www.jwmt.org/v2n17/gurney.html (accessed November 28, 2012).

Jacobs, Louis. *The Schocken Book of Jewish Mystical Testimonies: Compiled and with Commentary*. New York: Schocken Books, 1996.

James, William. *A Pluralistic Universe: Hibbert Lectures on the Present Situation in Philosophy*. 1996 Bison Books Paperback edition. Lincoln: University of Nebraska Press, 1909.

Jaron, Gary M. *Find Your Way*. unpublished manuscript, 2018.

Jewish Publication Society. *The Holy Scriptures according to the Masoretic Text: A new translation with the aid of previous versions and with constant consultation of Jewish authorities*. 1955 new edition. Edited by M L Margolis. Philadelphia: Jewish Publication Society, 1917.

Kaplan, Aryeh. *Sefer Yetzirah, The Book of Creation: In Theory and Practice.*

 Revised Edition 1997. York Beach: Samuel Weiser Inc., 1990.

—. *The Bahir (Illumination): Translation, Introduction and Commentary.* First

 Paperback edition 1989. Translated by Aryeh Kaplan. York Beach:

 Samuel Weiser, Inc., 1979.

Kupperman, J. S. "Tarot and Kabbalistic Sacred Geometry." *Journal of the*

 Western Mystery Tradition 2, no. 17 (2009): 1-19.

Kushner, Lawrence. *The Way Into Jewish Mystical Tradition.* Woodstock:

 Jewish Lights Publishing, 2001.

Levenson, Jon D. *Creation and the Persistence of Evil: The Jewish Drama of Divine*

 Omnipotence. First Princeton Paperback Edition 1994. Princeton,

 New Jersey: Princeton University Press, 1988.

Levi, Eliphas. *The Book of Splendours: The Inner Mysteries of Qabalism Its*

 relationship to Freemasonry, Numerology & Tarot. Third Paperback

 edition 1984. Edited by R. A. Gilbert. York Beach: Samuel Weiser,

 Inc., 1894.

—. *Transcendental Magic its Doctrine and Ritual.* Edited by Alfred Edward

 White. Translated by Alfred Edward White. London: Rider and

 Company, 1896.

Mathers, Samuel Liddell MacGregor, trans. *The Kabbalah Unveiled: Translated into English from the Latin version of Knorr von Rosenroth, and collated with the original Chaldee and Hebrew text.* Vol. Fifth Paperback printing 1997. York Beach: Samuel Weiser, Inc., 1887.

Matt, Daniel C., ed. *The Heart of Jewish Mysticism.* Translated by Daniel C. Matt. San Francisco: HarperSanFrancisco, 1995.

Oxford University Press. *Oxford English Dictionary.* Second Edition. Oxford: Oxford University Press, 2004.

Place, Robert M. *The Tarot: History, Symbolism, and Divination.* New York: Jeremy P. Tarcher/Penguin, 2005.

Regardie, Israel. *The Tree of Life: A Study of Magic.* Second Edition, 1994 Reprint. York Beach: Samuel Weiser, Inc., 1968.

Regardie, Israel, Chic Cicero, and Sandra Tabatha Cicero. *A Garden of Pomegranates: Edited and Annotated with new material: Skrying on the Tree of Life.* Third Edition 1999. Edited by Chic Cicero and Sandra Tabatha Cicero. St. Paul: Llewellyn Publications, 1970.

Revak, J W. *Etteilla: The First Specifically Esoteric Tarot Deck.* November 03, 2001. http://www.villarevak.org/bio/etteilla_2.html (accessed November 24, 2012).

"Revived   Qabala."   *Psyche.com.*   January   1997.

www.psyche.com/psyche/qbl/revivedqabala.html   (accessed

September 09, 2012).

Scholem, Gershom G. *Alchemy and Kabbalah.* First English Translation 2006.

Translated by Klaus Ottmann. Putnam: Spring Publishers, Inc.,

1977.

—. *Kabbalah.* 1978 Paperback edition. New York: A Meridian Book, 1974.

—. *Major Trends in Jewish Mysticism.* Seventh Printing of Third Revised

Edition. New York: Schocken Books, 1954.

—. *On The Kabbalah and Its Symbolism.* Second Paperback Edition 1970.

Translated by Ralph Manheim. New York: Schocken Books, 1965.

Sperling, Harry, and Maurice Simon, *The Zohar.* Vol. One. Five vols. London:

The Soncino Press, 1931.

Stolzenberg, Daniel. "Four Trees, Some Amulets and the Seventy-two

Names of God: Kircher Reveals the Kabbalah." In *Athanasius Kircher:*

The Last Man Who Knew Everything, by Paula Findien, 143-164. New

York: Routledge, 2004.

Tishby, Isaiah, and Fischel Lachower. *The Wisdom of the Zohar: An Anthology*

of Texts, with extensive introductions and explanations. English

Translation edition 1983. Translated by David Goldstein. Vol. One.

Three vols. London: the Littman Library of Jewish Civilization, 1949.

Tolkien, J. R. R. *The Lord of the Rings.* 2004 50th Anniversary Edition. Vols. I, The Fellowship of the Ring. III vols. New York: Houghton Mifflin Company, 1954-1955.

Tripp, Edward. *The Meridian Handbook of Classical Mythology: Originally published as Crowell's Handbook of Classical Mythology.* New York: Meridian Book, 1974.

Waite, Arthur Edward. *The Holy Kabbalah: A Study of the Secret Tradition in Israel.* Oracle reprint 1996. Hertfordshire: Oracle Publishing, Inc., 1924.

Watts, Alan, and Chung-Huang Al. *Tao: the Watercourse Way.* New York: Pantheon Press, 1977.

Welch, Holmes. *Taoism: The Parting of the Way.* Boston: Beacon Press, 1966.

Wescott, William Wynn, trans. *Sepher Yetzirah or The Book of Creation: A translation of the Latin text of John Stephen Rittangel.* 1887.

Westcott, William Wynn. "An Introduction to the Study of the Kabbalah by William Wynn Westcott based on lectures." *Hermetic Order of the Golden Dawn.* 1910.

http://www.hermeticgoldendawn.org/hogdframeset.html

(accessed February 12, 2013).

Made in the USA
Columbia, SC
10 June 2022